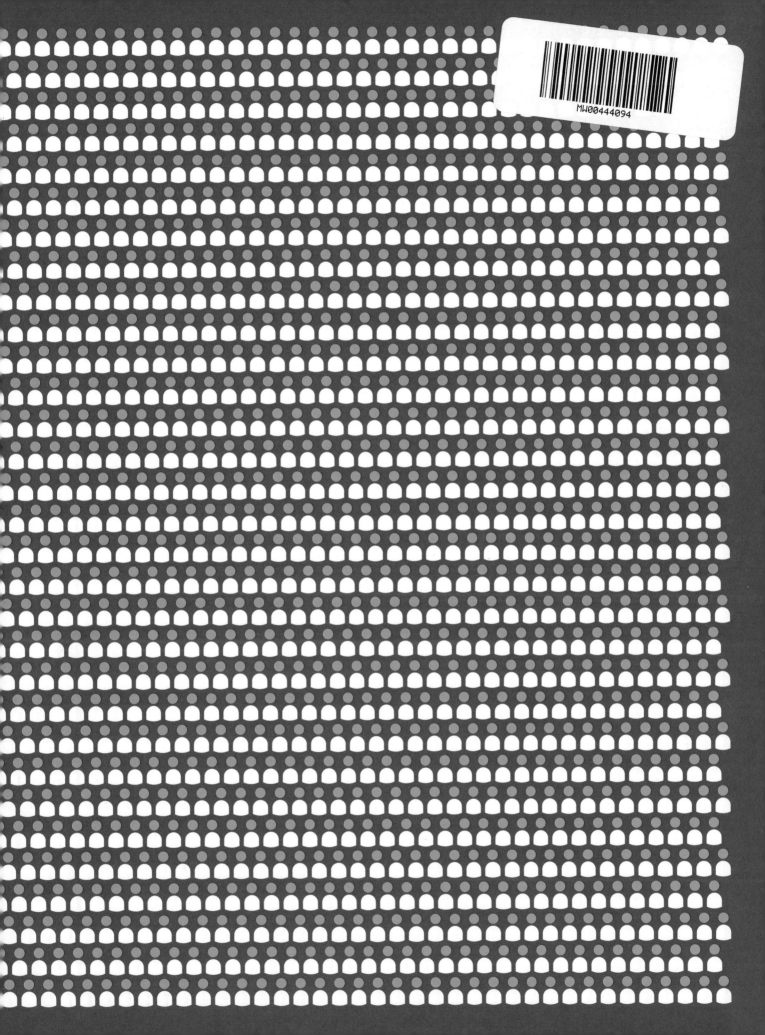

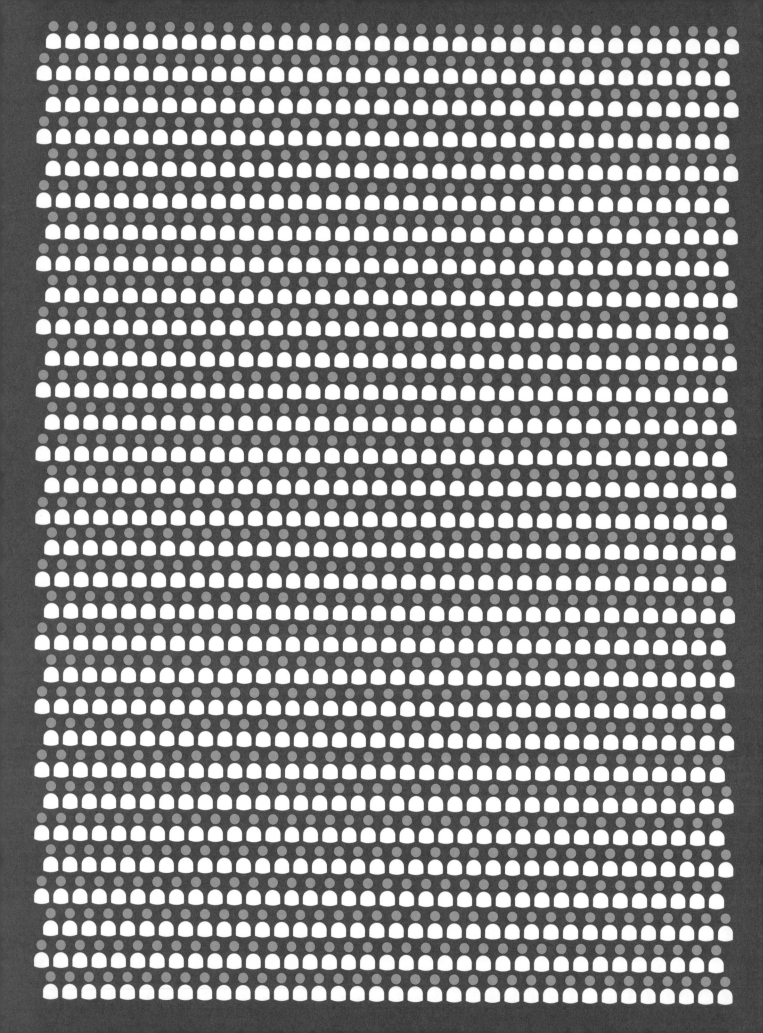

Designing
B2B Brands

Cover design: Carlos Martinez Onaindia and Nick Eagleton

This book is printed on acid-free paper.

Copyright © 2013 Deloitte Global Services Limited.

Published by John Wiley & Sons, Inc., Hoboken, New Jersey
Published simultaneously in Canada

Library of Congress Cataloging-in-Publication Data:

Martinez Onaindia, Carlos.
  Designing B2B brands : lessons from Deloitte and 195,000 brand managers / Carlos Martinez Onaindia & Brian Resnick.
    p. cm.
    Includes index.
    ISBN 978-1-118-45747-4 (cloth); ISBN 978-1-118-55443-2 (ebk); ISBN 978-1-118-55733-4 (ebk); ISBN 978-1-118-55763-1 (ebk)
    1. Branding (Marketing)–Management. 2. Brand name products–Management. 3. Corporate image. 4. Logos (Symbols)–Design. 5. Trademarks–Design. I. Resnick, Brian, 1974- II. Title.
  HF5415.1255.M374 2013
  658.8'27–dc23
                                                                2012039446

Printed in the United States of America

10 9 8 7 6 5 4 3 2 1

Designing
B2B Brands

Lessons from Deloitte
and 195,000 brand managers

Carlos Martínez Onaindía
& Brian Resnick

WILEY

Driving the brand (Belgium)
Deloitte Belgium is one of the country's main employers, and approximately 700 new employees are hired every year. An increasingly mobile and selective workforce is making attracting and retaining that talent more and more challenging. In September 2008, Deloitte Belgium welcomed its newest class of recent graduates and held a special event at which they met some of their new colleagues and were introduced to the firm. The introduction was most notable for its conclusion: at the end of the day, each of the newcomers received keys to their very own Deloitte-branded Mini Cooper car. Following the screening of a promotional film featuring hundreds of the cars touring the streets of Brussels (shot from a helicopter) and group participation in a safe-driving course, the new hires departed with a new car and a new appreciation for the organization they had joined. The initiative was rolled out in 2008, but juniors who start at Deloitte Belgium still receive a Mini and color the streets of Belgium.

Coming together to stand apart
A global Brand and Marketing Council is represented by nearly 50 Deloitte member firm leaders. In addition to their local roles, they come together periodically to shape the global direction of the brand.

Thank you

The visibility and strength of any business-to-business brand is first and foremost attributable to its people. That's why this book is dedicated to the 195,000 people of the Deloitte member firm network. The daily efforts of this diverse international collection of auditors, tax managers, consultants, and service professionals are directly responsible for shaping the brand. By defining and delivering on Deloitte's brand promise, they are able to take the biggest of ideas and make them real and relevant on an individual basis.

Within this 195,000 is a far smaller number of brand, marketing, and communications experts who focus heavily on overseeing the activation of the brand at the local level. Equal parts brand owners and stewards, this group has taken Deloitte's identity system and given it life across more than 100 countries. We thank them sincerely.

The Champions
Alexandre, Didier (France)
Allum, Lawrence (Australia)
Barrett, William J (USA)
Benko, Cathy (USA)
Berlusconi, Antonella (Italy)
Bihler, Birgit (Germany)
Bocart, Vincent (France)
Bodnarchuk, Tracey (Canada)
Bovopoulos, Bill (Australia)
Breunig, Samuel G (USA)
Casado, Jorge (Spain)
Cernich, Michal (Czech Republic)
Chang, Janet (USA)
Chico, Jennifer (USA)
Chopra, Jyoti (USA)
Currey, Shane (Australia)
De Keulenaer, Ludo (Belgium)
Delventhal, Anne C (UK)
De Maeyer, Marc (Belgium)
Den Held, Helen (Netherlands)
Dhawan, Atul (India)
Donald, Allan (Canada)
Espinosa, Andres (Colombia)
Estebanez, Jose Maria (Spain)
Evans, Roger (UK)
Farrall, Frank (Australia)
Freedman, Sue (USA)
Fuentes, Christian (Chile)
Fugere, Brian (USA)
Fyfe, Stasha M (UK)
Gallardo, Luis (USA)
Garcia, Julieta (Mexico)
Gatti, Virginia (Argentina)
Grabish, Michael (USA)
Graham, Dominic X (UK)
Gylfe, Suzanne (USA)
Haddad, Nada (Lebanon)
Hamilton, Toni (Australia)
Handy, Tamika (USA)
Heasley, Stephen (USA)
Howell, Matt (Czech Republic)
Hugo, Andre (South Africa)
Hutchinson, Jason D (Australia)
James, Andrew (UK)
Jensen, Frode Vik (Norway)
Jevtani, Divyesh (USA)
Kallet, Pushpa (Singapore)
Kaul, Upasna (China)
Keller, John (USA)
Kessner, Karen (Germany)
Kikuchi, Sachiyo (Japan)
Kirch, Kent (USA)

Knight, Kareem (USA)
Kumar, Malika (India)
Lam, Rebecca (China)
Lazaro, Onita (China)
Lee, Michelle (Canada)
Li, Freda (Canada)
Llaca, Lucia (Spain)
MacGibbon, Alan (Canada)
MacKenzie, Amanda (Canada
Martin, Carlos (Spain)
Mathurin, Michelle (UK)
Matsumoto, Robyn (Canada)
McNamee, Eloise (UK)
Meyer-Berkhout, Jan (Germany)
Mitsue, Taka (Japan)
Montes, Heloisa Helena (Brazil)
Nair, Meena (India)
O'Gorman, Irene (Ireland)
O'Gorman, Vanessa (Ireland)
Ordenes Rivas, Astrid (UK)
Pang, Pam (China)
Paradis, Annick N. (Canada)
Pearson, David (USA)
Phillipps, Tim (Singapore)
Place, Alistair (UK)
Pritchard, Annabel (UK)
Redhill, David J (Australia)
Reoli, Eric M (USA)
Salhab, Rana (Lebanon)
Scheidler, Susan (Spain)
Schirmacher, Carla A. (Mexico)
Schonfeld, Samantha (USA)
Scott, Tracy (Canada)
Seguine, Holly (USA)
Soerrig, Charlotte (Denmark)
Somers, Victoria (Australia)
Souza, Renato (Brazil)
Spapens, Mireille (Netherlands)
Stratmann, Jan (Germany)
Swat, Katarzyna (Poland)
Taylor, Peter (UK)
Tehan, Anna (China)
Teo, Maureen (Singapore)
Thiruchelvam, Shruti (Australia)
Torres, Lorena A (Mexico)
Tudor-Owen, Stuart (South Africa)
Vander Kuur, Cindy K (USA)
Van Rooyen, Caroline (South Africa)
Von Hammerstein, Philippa (Germany)
Walton, James M (Singapore)
Weinstein, Michael (USA)
Weiss, Antje (Germany)
Whiting, John (UK)

Williams, Sarah (UK)
Wittenauer, Frank (USA)
Zeeshan, Muhammad (USA)

The DTTL Global Brand team
Heather Hancock
Brian Resnick
Pia DeVitre
Alexander Hamilton
Gabriela Salinas
Carlos Martínez Onaindía
Cameron MacIntosh
Karla Anguiano
Joannie Sauvageau
Shruti Thiruchelvam
Marcie Richardson
Tracey Guzman
Lucy Chacon
Hunter Kaplan

The Guru
Alina Wheeler, author

Our publishing team at John Wiley & Sons
Amanda Miller, vice president and publisher
Margaret Cummins, executive editor
Michael New, editorial assistant
Kerstin Nasdeo, senior production manager
Justin Mayhew, associate marketing director
Penny Makras, marketing manager
David Sassian, senior production editor
Andrew Miller, copyeditor

And perpetual gratitude to our agency, The Partners, for their creativity and brilliance, and for helping us to continue daily to shape the Deloitte brand
Jim Prior, CEO
Nick Eagleton, creative director
Andrew Webster, client director
And the rest of The Partners' team

There are 195,000 professionals around the world actively shaping the Deloitte identity on a daily basis. Brand-building of that scale requires relentless focus on a unified vision and shared values, alongside a dynamic culture. There's tremendous opportunity if you get this right.

BARRY SALZBERG
Chief Executive Officer
Deloitte Touche Tohmatsu Limited

Welcome

Business can only fully realise the power of its brand when it has a clear and relevant system for aligning purpose, actions, and results. The infiltration of consumerist behaviour into B2B relationships demands that we up our game in leveraging our brand value. Deloitte is an advisory business whose brand relies on the daily actions of nearly 200,000 people in more than 150 countries being connected and reflecting the same core commitments. We begin with a unifying ideal, a clear sense of the impact we wish to achieve. We connect our people and our brand in myriad ways, always informed by a deep understanding of the marketplace and our clients' needs. And we take the long view, remaining committed to the task at hand whilst building value for clients and our own firm long into the future. It delivers us client and personal growth, risk insulation, and trust.

I hope you find this book a useful guide as you shape and strengthen your own brand to accelerate meeting your business ambitions.

HEATHER HANCOCK
Global Managing Partner, Brand
Deloitte Touche Tohmatsu Limited

How to use this book

There are lots of books on branding. And lots of those books are really, really good. Most focus on consumer brands: cans on shelves, mascot elves—stuff like that. Search hard enough and you'll also find a few brand books on business-to-business, well, businesses. Perhaps not surprisingly, there's loads of theory in those. Some case studies. A handful of best practices. Useful.

But those books are not this book. This book is different. Also useful. But different.

This is the story of a system. A global system. Built by a dozen or so people. Then used by 195,000 people. And now experienced by millions of people. In roughly the same way. Same, in this case, is not a bad thing. That sameness is not a boring or a bland thing. It's a brand thing. It actually helps to bring revenue to the balance sheet. Helps to bring people together. Helps to bring meaning to lives.

OK, now here's where it gets really good: this system… it's replicable. And because just one very, very big global brand is spotlighted, it will be clear how all the many, many moving parts work together.

You, the B2B brand and marketing professional, can use this model. Use it to make your brand stronger, your identity system more sustainable. A B2B business executive? Read and learn how your brand stewardship can inspire. Are you a designer? See how to maximize your creative in a controlled corporate environment. Work at an agency? Identify areas to contribute to, adding key external perspectives. Business school student? Gain a deep understanding of how leading brands are formed and maintained, and how you can enrich them.

See, we're all brand managers. No matter what it says on your business card or resume. We present ideas, represent ideals. Shape and share experiences. With every touch-point, every interaction. Use this book to help make them connect. Use this book to help make them count.

Timesavers

Throughout the book you will find a large number of gray text boxes with representative category symbols. Within each is a list containing an assortment of reminders, recommendations, alerts, and rewards. They are points of emphasis to steer your B2B brand-building efforts in the right direction.

 Insights

 Watch out

 Top tips

 Consider

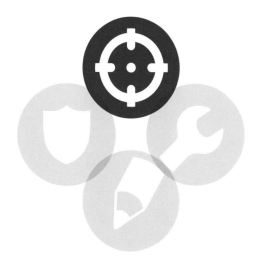

Section 1:
Defining it
Brand overview

What is branding, and why is it more important than ever? Before a global business-to-business brand can be built, its true meaning, reach, and value must be fully understood.

Section 2:
Building it
Brand elements

The core components of a corporate identity will shape every single piece of communication, guaranteeing clarity and consistency. The strength and compatibility of these design elements is directly correlated to the impact of the brand.

Section 3:

Using it

Brand applications

Successful global systems are flexible, allowing for extensions of all brand elements while retaining consistency. Understanding and planning for every channel and vehicle of connectivity is critical.

Section 4:

Defending it

From alliance to compliance

No matter how strong the system, its effectiveness is ultimately determined by the active management of a centralized team, in concert with a globally shared desire to foster the brand.

Brand overview

What is branding, and why is it more important than ever? Before a global business-to-business brand can be built, its true meaning, reach, and value must be fully understood.

Defining it

What is branding?

Culture... Attributes... Values... Design... Identity... Symbols... People... Stories... Relationships... Perception. Speak to ten business professionals and you'll hear ten different ideas concerning the essence of branding. Ironically, what tends to get left out—confidence, clarity, and consistency—is exactly what is most needed to build a successful brand.

All of the above words are valid, if incomplete, descriptors of branding. When taken together, however, organized into a model, and aligned with a business strategy, the ideas they represent become something far greater than their sum. They become a potent mix of the tangible and intangible, the experienced and the anticipated. They can influence behavior and differentiate one organization from another.

The Deloitte brand was born in 2003, when a loosely knit network of accounting, tax, and advisory firms fused in name, mission, and spirit. Since then, the global brand has grown organically and acquisitively, and the organization has come to be recognized as an industry leader. In 2010, the Deloitte member firms comprised the world's largest professional-services network. Propelling this growth has been a unified vision: to be "the standard of excellence." While revenue and headcounts are obviously important, the brand vision is focused on member firms being the first choice of the world's most sought-after clients and talent. It is believed that only this goal and the collective journey required to achieve it will enable the Deloitte brand to find itself a category of one. It is an idea, and an ideal, that drives the organization and fosters brand distinction.

If you're confused, don't dismay: even academics and industry gurus struggle to explain branding. Most lean on the concept of "trust" or, more commonly, "a promise"—a promise to stakeholders built on consistency and quality of product and service, people and culture. But what if the product or service has never been purchased? If the people and culture have never been encountered? For successfully branded businesses, it doesn't matter, because branding is more than just a promise. Branding is faith.

If that takes things in a direction that is a little spiritual—a bit, dare we say, religious—it is not by accident. (Look no further than the topical lexicon, which is peppered with terms such as "brand evangelists," "brand beliefs," and "preaching the brand." It is even quite common for corporate visual-identity guidebooks to be referred to as "brand bibles"!) Nor is it something to be scared by or dismissive of. Understanding and embracing the essence of an organization is at the heart of branding. And finding value and meaning in the essence of an organization, even without having experienced all it is and all it has to offer, is the faith that leads to business success.

Lacking faith?

Here are ten reasons for B2B brand investment:

1. **Reputation strengthening.** Community-driven association and validation, highlighted by the realization of a halo effect for any brand-related assets

2. **Risk mitigation.** The reduction of uncertainty and potential liabilities through definition, reconciliation, and reinforcement of core qualities and assets

3. **Client-building.** Clarifying business benefits, embedding advance impressions in the client base that are both positive and organic

4. **Workforce enhancement.** Contributing to an organization's culture while building loyalty and pride, thereby assisting with talent acquisition and retention

5. **Focused messaging.** Creating a foundation underpinning all oral and written communications, leading to a singular voice and desirable reactions

6. **Information efficiency.** Enabling a clearer and more coordinated product and services offer

7. **Merger and acquisition facilitation.** Organizational reputation and positioning that attracts and expedites negotiation and closing

8. **Increased market capitalization.** The correlation between targeted brand investment and business growth rate

9. **Driving financial performance.** Qualitative and quantitative support for the fiscal benefits of strategic brand management

10. **Activating a purpose.** The defining reason for existing that extends beyond the bottom line and provides necessary meaning to all who interact with the brand

What is brand identity?

Brand identity is common sense: a codified collection of shared elements (things in common) that are activated through a range of visual, verbal, and aural qualities (elements of sense). And common sense is what's needed to distinguish today's B2B brands.

Branding is not brand identity—though to speak to the vast majority of business professionals, you'd think they were one and the same. To be fair, the confusion is understandable. Brand identity is expressed through the most physically embodied aspects of the organization. It is the manifestation of the brand that can be seen, heard, and immediately experienced. The strongest B2B brand identities, not unlike those belonging to people, are comprised of many integrated and deeply realized attributes, given life through consistent and considered application. As part of a strategically integrated system of design and communication, the brand identity has the ability to impress and imprint, to distinguish the organization and build an appetite for future interaction.

The other popular misconception is that "brand identity" and "visual identity" can be used interchangeably. This is like saying that pizza is cheese. Ingredients may have stand-alone value, but in combination they are but elements of a whole and total creation. Brand identity encompasses visual identity, aural identity, and the other sensory components of a brand. B2Bs express themselves with more than just visuals; they use written and spoken words, the reception of which can be directed through contextual cues and tone of voice. Sonic palettes guide the auditory properties of the brand and are commonly brought to life in corporate marketing and multimedia vehicles. Some B2B brands—yes, B2B brands—even associate their organization with certain smells.

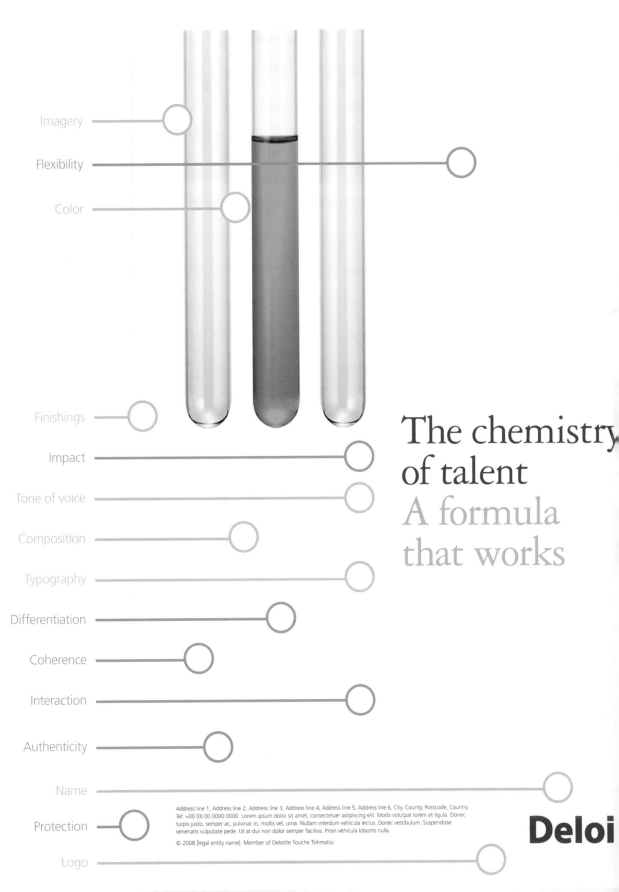

Elements of chemistry
The Deloitte brand identity is epitomized by a focused, straightforward presentation. This is made possible by a suite of flexible core elements that work together to communicate through a mix of intelligence and vibrancy.

Imagery

Flexibility

Color

Finishings

Impact

Tone of voice

Composition

Typography

Differentiation

Coherence

Interaction

Authenticity

Name

Protection

Logo

The chemistry of talent
A formula that works

Address line 1, Address line 2, Address line 3, Address line 4, Address line 5, Address line 6, City, County, Postcode, Country
Tel: +00 (0) 00 0000 0000 Lorem ipsum dolor sit amet, consectetuer adipiscing elit. Morbi volutpat lorem et ligula. Donec turpis justo, semper ac, pulvinar in, mollis vel, urna. Nullam interdum vehicula lectus. Donec vestibulum. Suspendisse venenatis vulputate pede. Ut at dui non dolor semper facilisis. Proin vehicula lobortis nulla.

© 2008 [legal entity name]. Member of Deloitte Touche Tohmatsu

Deloi

The year 2013 marks the ten-year anniversary of the Deloitte brand. When the network of member firms officially coalesced, although there was considerable retention of their individual cultures, attributes, and even operating models, there was at the same time an immediate and palpable shift around the new common brand identity. Its rapid adoption was driven not only by the more tangible, identifiable nature of the visual assets, but also by a highly integrated design and communication system that provided a shared tonality and personality across geographic, cultural, and functional borders. Member firms saw this as a way to connect to something bigger and better and to deliver a unified Deloitte experience.

The Deloitte brand identity system is always evolving, endeavoring to stay fresh and relevant to member firms and their audiences. Launched in 2003 and recipient of a systemwide refresh in 2008, the brand is continually evaluated by the Global Brand team of Deloitte Touche Tohmatsu Limited. The team assesses the thousands of bespoke brand assets, updating and retooling them for optimal use and end-user experience. Guidelines are also frequently enhanced, with periodic "gap analyses" identifying new areas in which to define the Deloitte presence. Most recently, additions resulting from such assessments have included mobile app interfaces, infographics, and "wordmarks," which visually represent signature programs and initiatives.

DeepDive™
The ultimate collaboration tool

DeepDive™ turns every business meeting into a high-energy, high-productivity event. DeepDive™ takes important problems and helps teams create solutions fast – often in hours instead of weeks.

www.deloitte.com

"Aha" begins here
DeepDive™

DeepDive™ turns every business meeting into a high-energy, high-productivity event. DeepDive™ takes important problems and helps teams create solutions fast – often in hours instead of weeks.

www.deloitte.com

To get the right answers, we help you to ask the right questions
DeepDive™

DeepDive™ turns every business meeting into a high-energy, high-productivity event. DeepDive™ takes important problems and helps teams create solutions fast – often in hours instead of weeks.

www.deloitte.com

Deloitte.

Deloitte.

Deloitte.

Going even deeper
"Deep Dive™" is a proprietary process focused on the strategic identification of problems and the construction of solutions. The essential aspect of immersion is thematically articulated in the process's visual identity; here, traditional office supplies are shown in a submerged state.

I wanted a brand identity that consistently captured the hearts and minds of our people and clients. Through many different analytic lenses, the simple and striking visual concept of "inside out" captures the essence of our common vision.

TIM PHILLIPPS
Global Leader, Deloitte Analytics
Deloitte Touche Tohmatsu Limited

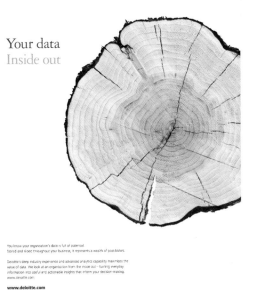

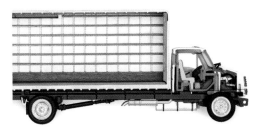

An inside view of identities
Just as the Deloitte master brand possesses an identity, so, too, do its many groups, programs, and offerings. One of the best examples is Deloitte Analytics, a multinational service line that provides data analysis expertise. Its ability to look deeper is dynamically and distinctly expressed through images of cross-sectioned objects, all paired with "inside out" verbal theming.

B2B versus B2C branding

Whereas business-to-consumer brand purchases are often made on impulse, business-to-business decisions are driven by myriad factors and can span many months. So for B2Bs, think "best to build": brand embedding requires significant investment, spread over numerous touch-points, over an expanse of time.

As with the services and solutions they provide, there is much nuance and complexity in how B2B providers go about building brand loyalty. Although the internet has provided purchasing audiences with access to more information than ever before, decisions about B2C brands still generally require far less research than those about B2Bs. This increased scrutiny, coupled with typically extended negotiations involving multiple decision makers, can exponentially lengthen the B2B brand selection process.

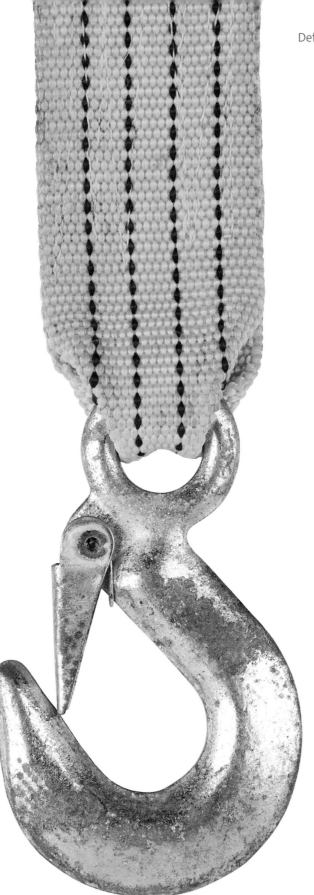

Deloitte has 195,000 skilled professionals actively shaping its brand. In many ways, those professional services providers are the brand. B2B is viewed as P2P—people to people—and Deloitte member firm professionals offer personal knowledge, insights, and experience. With a holistic understanding of and approach to the branding needed, topical training is provided worldwide to educate Deloitte professionals about its importance and function. This helps ensure that the brand is delivered (and not just from a marketing and communications standpoint) with consistency and quality.

The sheer number of criteria driving the choice of a B2B provider presents an organization with ample opportunities to influence an audience. It is critical that businesses understand the highly strategic mindset of their stakeholders and respond in an insightful and incisive manner, adopting a comprehensive approach to managing all touch-points. Each interaction offers a number of chances to fortify—or, if mishandled, weaken—the B2B brand and the business's value proposition. The mapping of related touch-points is an advisable exercise, helping to align distinct audiences and needs with targeted messages and vehicles. Such plotting can ensure that the business is well-positioned to consistently shape the experiences of current and prospective clients, recruits, shareholders, analysts, and even employees.

Which leads to the one other key differentiator, and it really is the embodiment of B2B branding: people. They are not only at the heart of a business but serve as its eyes, ears, and mouth. They are the driving force behind the interaction with all relevant audiences. They use communication to lead to connectivity, to lead to brand awareness, to lead to brand experience, to lead to brand loyalty. This degree of personal representation is completely absent from nearly all B2Cs.

The following tips are specific to B2B brands.
They are designed to help a business foster relationships and enhance its eminence and reputation.

- **Make a difference by being different.** In a highly commoditized marketplace, saying you are distinct is different than showing you are distinct. Achieve authentic cut-through more easily by amplifying key distinguishing characteristics at all touch-points.

- **Get working on networking.** Take advantage of meeting and speaking opportunities as well as both organic and manufactured occasions to dialogue via social media in order to forge relationships.

- **Go beyond the personal touch to add a touch of personality.** Storytelling—anecdotal evidence of brand activation, delivered by internal and external stakeholders—can add authenticity and foster enhanced connectivity.

- **Content management is brand management.** Some of the best B2B brands are the best producers of informative, innovative thought leadership. Leverage available media channels to remain in front of the audience.

- **Open doors with endorsements.** Third-party testimonials, promoted on external websites, blogs, and social channels, can be useful proof points in soliciting clients and recruiting new hires.

The "brandscape"

It is occupied by all products, people, organizations, and innovations. Its study is a customary part of the curriculum for MFAs as well as MBAs. Its mapping is a crucial component of business strategy, addressed not just by CMOs but by CEOs as well. It is alluded to on style sheets and balance sheets alike. Truly, the brand of branding has never been stronger.

Brands—especially those in the B2B space—are better understood and more fully realized than ever before. Businesses and customers alike recognize that brands extend beyond logos, taglines, and advertising. The value exchange that they promise drives relationships, drives reputation, and drives results. Today's brands inspire and incite action more than the promoted products and services of yesterday ever could because they represent more than the products and services of yesterday ever could.

What can we expect in the years to come? The brand future will be far more clearly linked to our shared future. There will be continued evolution from the packaging of goods to the packaging of good and ever greater focus on societal benefit. Brand-building efforts will be amplified by new channels of connectivity, and not just "traditional" social media (if such a word can be used to describe platforms still in their relative infancy).

In this new world of tailored marketing and a plethora of communications channels, the brand experience is now an intensely personal experience, and just showing your logo to the masses no longer cuts it. In every industry, the brandscape is increasingly about the quality and intelligence of your branding and less about the quantity and the big-budget advertising approach of the past.

JAMES WALTON
Clients & Markets Director
Deloitte Singapore & Southeast Asia

Emerging markets like Southeast Asia and Africa will not only influence the positioning of global brands but will also produce highly regarded global brands of their own. And all successful B2B brands will be "experience" brands, defined not by their products and services but by intangible and emotional triggers activated at every touch-point.

Brand strategy

Understanding brand strategy begins with understanding business strategy. The commercial and social imperatives of an organization are what ultimately define the brand, and a clear brand strategy enables those drivers to be articulated and activated consistently and compellingly.

"Brand strategy" is a term often used interchangeably with "brand positioning," "brand promise," and "brand identity," not to mention—sadly—"marketing strategy." The confusion is dangerous, as it can limit the effectiveness of an organization's brand-building efforts. As with each of the other terms, this one has a clear and specific meaning. And as with most strategies, brand strategy is a high-level connecter, driver, and enabler; it aggregates the core properties of a business and neatly shapes them into a mechanism for delivering the who, what, where, why, and how of the brand.

The process begins not with brand alignment but with business alignment. Once the latter is achieved, the former can be coordinated. Brand objectives should be defined, target audience determined, and potential obstacles identified. Only then should the identity and imprinting efforts begin. This manner of staged, iterative brand-building guarantees a model that is both systemic and authentic—two qualities critical to success. Branding consistently, compellingly, and strategically will lead directly to better brand equity, and brand equity translates directly to brand value and the ability to charge a premium for products and services.

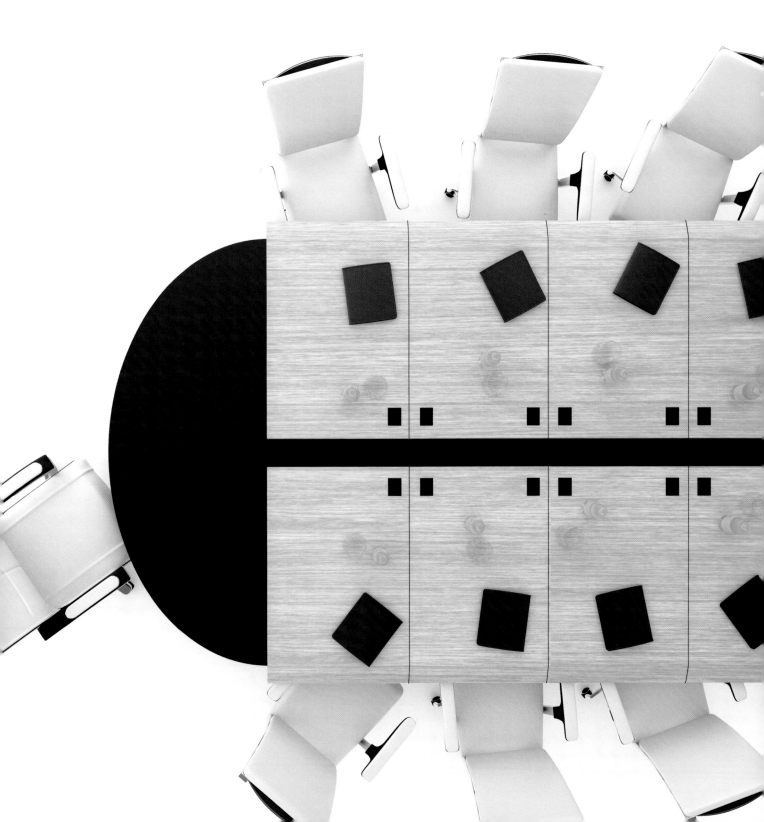

Deloitte's brand strategy centers on being the first choice of the world's most sought-after clients and talent. This ambition is realized through an organization-wide focus on delivering a suite of experiential attributes. Of course, this places great responsibility and emphasis on the people of the Deloitte member firms—necessary, considering the highly commoditized, relationship-driven nature of the professional services industry.

Just as the Deloitte brand is viewed differently depending on its position in the local marketplace, so, too, is the brand strategy defined and activated in ways appropriate to local conditions. The network supports a degree of member firm flexibility, which is needed to bring the master-brand to life with relevance and resonance.

> For a brand to have impact it has to speak to you and create an emotional attachment. It must have a strong foundation, built on authenticity, and be true to its people, clients, and marketplace.

ALAN MACGIBBON
Global Managing Director, Quality, Strategy & Communications
Deloitte Touche Tohmatsu Limited

The 7 key questions for developing a B2B brand strategy:

1. **What is the current perception of the organization?** Current reputation, audience views of what is offered and how, existing differentiators.

2. **What is the desired perception of the organization?** Future associations and points of recognition, aspirations.

3. **What is the competitive landscape?** Existing brands that may already be entrenched, provide barriers to entry, are better resourced.

4. **Is there sufficient cross-function/ cross-service/cross-border consistency?** Alignment needed for common views, common culture, common positioning.

5. **How mature is the legacy brand positioning?** Degree of work required to alter existing perceptions, positive impressions to build upon.

6. **Is there leadership support?** Executive understanding and ambassadorship; willingness to align ability, to prioritize, and to sync with business goals.

7. **What resources are available?** For any competitive pricing strategies, organizational growth, for marketing and promotion of brand.

Brand architecture

Brand-building, like home-building, requires careful design. It calls for a strong foundation, optimal use of the allotted space, and sensitivity to the surrounding environment. It must reflect the personality of the owners and allow for future expansion. No matter the brilliance of the brand strategy, without an adequate architecture, the entire effort is destined to fail.

Brand architecture is not just for B2Cs and consumer product naming. It is arguably even more important for B2Bs to have a clearly defined structure for all functions and services within their brand portfolios, especially given the intangibility of the products and a general lack of perceived differentiation. That said, the architecture is not simply for clarifying hierarchy or emphasizing core offerings. It also makes possible the labeling and clustering of all assets logically and palatably. Local business units, service-line extensions, marcom programs, and apps and other electronic properties are just some of the areas given form and familiarity by brand architecture.

Brand architecture
Overview

Level	Item	Description / example
	Membership organization	Deloitte Touche Tohmatsu Limited
1b	**Member firm name**	e.g. UK member firm: Deloitte LLP US member firm: Deloitte LLP Japan member firm: Tohmatsu
1c	**Subsidiary legal entity**	e.g. Deloitte & Touche Tax Technologies LLP
	Master brand	**Deloitte**
	Functions	Audit Consulting Financial Advisory Tax
	Market offers	Enterprise Risk Services Merger & Acquisition Services Sustainability & Climate Change IFRS Growth Enterprise Services (Middle market) Analytics
	Industry programs & segments	Consumer business and transportation Energy and resources Financial services Life sciences and healthcare Manufacturing Public sector Real Estate Technology, media and telecommunications
	Proprietary products & tools	e.g. DeepDive™ Enterprise Value Map™ Culture Print™ Audit Plus™
	Brand initiatives	e.g. Technology Fast500 EngageD Impact Day Deloitte University Deloitte21 Canadian Asian Network (CAN)
	Branded acquisitions	e.g. Drivers Jonas Deloitte Recap ClearCarbon
	Sponsorships & endorsements	e.g. Olympics Royal Opera House, London

Labels (left): Membership organization, Master brand, Company divisions, Services, Programs and segments, Proprietary products and tools, Proprietary initiatives, Sub-brands, Endorsed brands

Traditionally, there have been three commonly cited types of architectural systems: monolithic brands, dominated by a singular corporate name grafted onto all components under the company umbrella; endorsed brands, featuring a family of sub-brands aligned by some sort of explicit endorsement or association; and freestanding brands, whose products and services have distinct identities and whose affiliation with a parent company, if any, is implicit. However, new business complexities have brought with them new stratifications of brand architecture. A more detailed and sophisticated modeling process—identifying the specific benefits and shortcomings of alternative arrangements—is required in order to effectively structure today's B2B brands.

The Deloitte brand architecture is an organization-wide framework that helps to present the global brand and all it represents in a coordinated and consistent way. It makes explicit the relationship between the Deloitte brand and the various services and proprietary products and tools on offer and harmonizes diverse brand-building initiatives. Adhering to the architecture clarifies to both clients and talent the level at which they approach the organization and just what capabilities are available.

At the heart of the brand architecture are a few key decisions, none more important than the avoidance of sub-brands. Nothing should ever dilute the strength and sovereignty of the Deloitte master brand. This construct allows for the fullest expression of the unique combination of qualities that is brought to stakeholders, a multidimensional offering, emphasizing a collaborative approach. It also enables the coherent presentation of a global organization to the audiences of member firms. And the brand architecture underlies the principles guiding the entire identity system. It is the basis of the communication and information hierarchy used in nearly all print and digital applications.

Architectural firm: Building a case for a sturdy brand architecture

- **Enhanced product scaling.** Client offerings and services are more easily recalibrated to accommodate business and marketplace shifts.

- **Reduced brand and marcom spend.** Structured clustering facilitates a more coordinated and cost-efficient positioning and promotional effort.

- **Operational alignment.** Harmonization of brand and business models, delivering optimal clarity for all stakeholders.

- **Identity shaping.** Connects business strategy to marcom strategy, feeding a design system more authentic to the organizational ethos.

- **Talent acclimation.** Clearer, more specific operations leading to rapid on-boarding and cultural absorption.

- **Talent retention and growth.** Well-defined hierarchy illustrating breadth of organization, as well as opportunities for lateral and upward professional transitions.

Types of brands

Master brand	Master-branded divisions	Master-branded personalities	Endorsed businesses	Endorsed brands	Freestanding brands
• Fewer resources spent on designing and protecting new logos/ sub-brands • Effectiveness built through the equity of one brand • Clarity about what the brand is, offers, and stands for • Brand awareness and preference built more easily in new and existing markets • Aligned internal understanding of the brand • Cost-efficient	• Fewer resources spent on designing and protecting new logos/ sub-brands • Distinction and credibility in markets or sectors where the brand is strong • Cultures cluster around the divisional brand rather than the core group brand • Divisional brands benefit from the development of equity	• Infrequently used, most progressive approach • Requires a strong parent brand • Fits with entrepreneurial businesses and brands diversified in their sector • Requires investment in each individual brand • Benefits from the parent group's halo effect • Marketplace failures well shielded from other brands • Expensive, sophisticated approach difficult to manage	• Result from growth through mergers and acquisitions • Retain their name but adopt the parent group's key visual elements • Build visual equity and a clear link to the group • Specific businesses maintain their sense of self • Footprint of a confederation of companies • Create internal conflict between group and local operation • Lack self-confidence and commitment to the group brand	• Deliver a distinct proposition but feature the stamp of the parent • Endorsements like adopting the parent brand name, using a signature of affiliation, et al. • Penetration of markets where the parent brand lacks credibility or relevance • Can lack clarity and strength	• Provide little indication of a relationship among them • More common among B2Cs than B2Bs • Segmented, complex marketplaces where brands compete with one another • Complicated and expensive to manage • Galvanize and align internally around the corporate brand, not the product brands

What's your "archi-type"?
Business and brand complexities have led to a more nuanced definition of architectural types. Six of the more common B2B systems are featured here.

The power of Deloitte's brand architecture is at the heart of our ability to go to market "As One." Our clients benefit from this integrated approach by being able to tap all aspects of our global architecture—from company divisions to services to programs and segments to proprietary products and tools—helping them address some of their most critical challenges.

JOHN LEVIS
Regional Managing Director, Americas; Managing Director, Global Integrated Market Offerings; and Chief Innovation Officer
Deloitte Touche Tohmatsu Limited

Brand purpose

Why do we exist? The question has been asked and the answer debated since the beginning of time. And just as it has caused great consternation for mankind, so, too, has it for "brand-kind." The search for purpose is the search for a true brand definer able to give meaning to an organization and all who work for and with it.

"Purpose" is one of the newest buzzwords to enter into both brand and business conversations. And with good reason. Purpose enables employees to understand why they are doing what they do every day. Ideally, purpose is more than just serving clients or building business revenue. While obviously important, these can become somewhat hollow, undifferentiated pursuits. Knowing the raison d'être of an organization is knowing one's own reason for being; such knowledge illuminates both role and, in every sense of the word, responsibility.

Branding with purpose

When working on the identification and promotion of purpose, keeping the following three concepts in mind will help you take a B2B brand from idea to ideal:

1. **Credibility.** Purpose must be authentic, true to the essence of the organization and all it stands for.

2. **Connectivity.** Purpose must be intuitively understood, clearly tied to business services.

3. **Communication.** Purpose must be embedded in business material, organically woven throughout internal and external vehicles.

Brand positioning

Make or take? With B2B brand positioning, it's either one or the other. Proactively make a statement about organizational differentiators, or reactively take what the audience ascribes to your brand. While the former can help carve a niche and set your business apart, the latter can damage any efforts to distinguish it.

In the B2B space, brand positioning can be succinctly defined as a "collective comparative" view of an organization, product, or service. It must effectively and authentically represent the whole while demonstrating how that aggregate stands apart from the competition. Unlike B2Cs, there is customarily a long relationship-building period, highlighted by numerous touch-points and decision-makers; all contribute to a lengthened positioning process.

When taking a stand on where a brand stands, begin by focusing on core attributes. These qualities, existent in the very fiber of the organization and its people, will help give any positioning a necessary grounding in what is real and relevant.

And much as the brand attributes are a mix of the immediate and the aspirational, so, too, is the brand positioning. Ideally, the positioning platform will be summarized by a simple slogan that is easily understood by all employees. When this understanding is converted into action, influencing behavior and experience, the brand will take on more meaning in the eyes, minds, and hearts of its audience.

Positioning the positioning
The Deloitte brand was featured at the 2011 World Economic Forum in Davos, Switzerland, as part of an anamorphic display. As the audience literally "stepped ahead," their altered perspective shaped a bold expression of the positioning statement.

The B2B world continues to see product/ service life cycles shrink, and the barriers/ costs to replication and copycatting fall. In this environment, a strong brand positioning takes on increased strategic prominence.

BRIAN FUGERE
Principal
Deloitte United States

"Always One Step Ahead" is the legacy brand positioning statement for Deloitte. It served as an organization-wide call to action. It inspired people, both individually and collectively, to contribute to realizing the global vision of becoming the standard of excellence. Of course, the Deloitte member firms and their people were not always Always One Step Ahead; it is impossible to be, in all markets and all situations. That is why the brand positioning statement was never treated as a tagline for an external audience: it could not be claimed with complete accuracy. It served more as a rallying cry—the benchmark that Deloitte member firm professionals used to filter and judge their own actions.

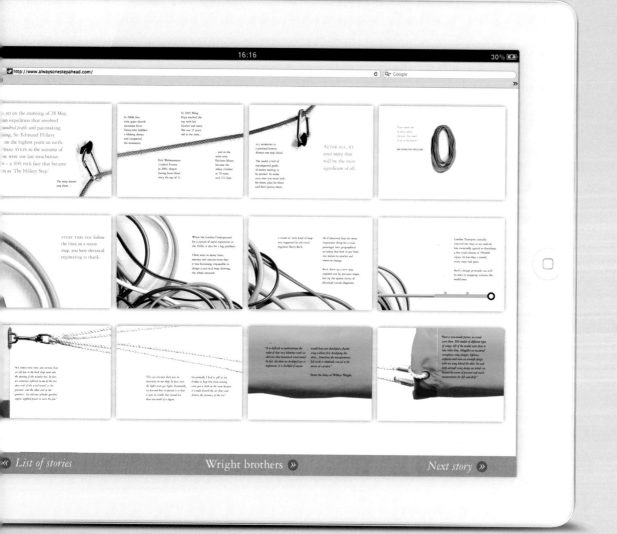

Inside-the-box thinking

As part of a brand positioning rollout, a "brand in a box" kit was created and delivered to everyone involved in marketing at a member firm. An attractive, easily consumable package housed key implements of brand activation: an overview leaflet, an inspirational film, and an attributes-focused storybook that included a global assortment of Always One Step Ahead tales, all implicitly linked to the legacy positioning.

AT 11.30 ON the morning of 28 May, after an expedition that involved *four hundred people* and painstaking planning, Sir Edmund Hillary stood on the highest point on earth. HIS FINAL STEPS to the summit of Everest were *one last treacherous climb* – a 40ft rock face that became known as *'The Hillary Step.'* The story doesn't stop there…

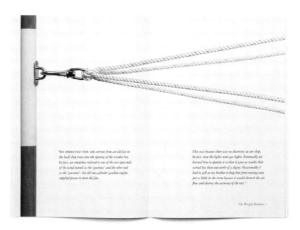

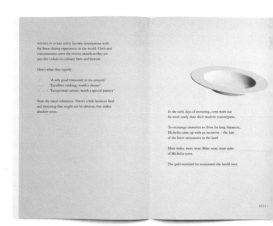

Brand experience

"Experience" is the word of the day, with dramatically increased audience touch-points and channels providing ample opportunity for brand interface and influence. For those B2Bs that embrace this idea and dedicate resources to delivering on their brand promises at all points of interaction, the experience of category leadership awaits.

The sum of all encounters that an individual has with a business—its people, products, and services—is the brand experience. Unlike the B2C brand experience, which is defined by a minimal number of immediate, acute sensations, B2B brand experience is notable for an extended time horizon and influences that are as nuanced as they are numerous.

The recent emphasis on digital channels has placed "user experience" in the spotlight; the term is now commonplace for online content sharing, design, and interface. It currently receives somewhat disproportionate attention, relative to brand experience. After all, user experience is simply the virtual brand experience.

Stakeholders filter

Channels filter

Brand touch-points

Popular best practices

Best practices
associated with each
touch-point

Submissions

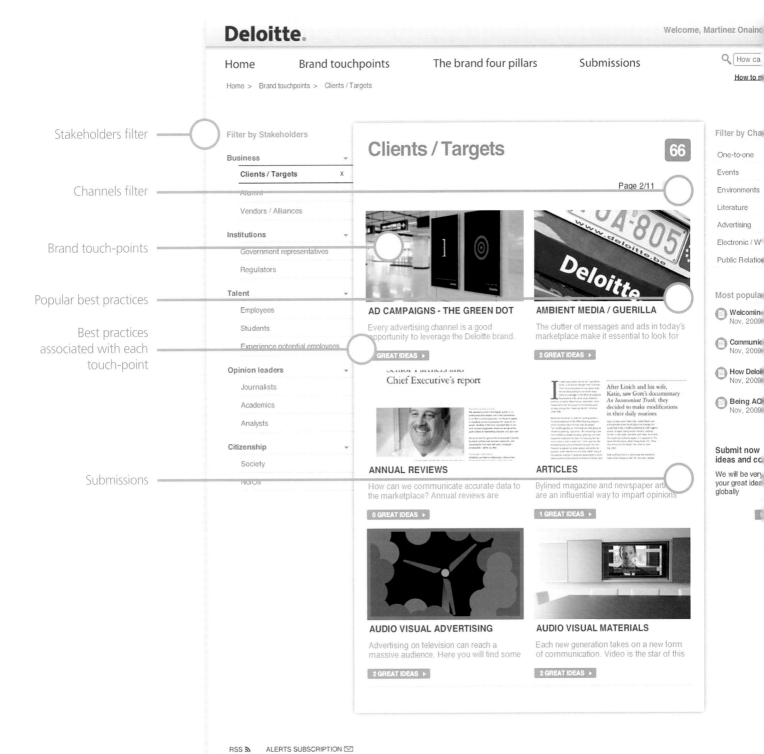

The Deloitte brand experience should reflect the organization's common values and differentiate it from the competition. This is achieved by leaning heavily on the brand attributes, thinking about them not just merely as internal signposts, but also as desired responses from all who interact with the brand. All clients and talent are thereby left with a consistently positive impression distinguished by the implicit benefits of inspiration, achievement, and support.

"Focus"—the brand personality—also factors mightily in the shaping of unmistakably Deloitte experiences. As so many of the touch-points have a visual orientation, including print and electronic pieces, events, and office materials, compositional and tonal consistency are critical. A focused approach strips away unnecessary elements, concentrates on audience needs, and imparts ideas in deeply meaningful ways.

Brand experience enhancers
Consider the following five methods for developing an experience brand:

1. **Know your ABCs.** Always Be Consistent. Focus on articulating brand characteristics to all those responsible for shaping and sharing organizational assets. This will provide a foundation for all interaction.

2. **Less is more.** Avoid overcustomization, and emphasize a few, preset core ideas. As services, products, and people change, the brand promise will remain the same.

3. **Selling by storytelling.** Stories that are personal, relevant, and compelling add humanity and richness to a brand, making experiences memorable and distinct.

4. **Value-add, multiplied.** Add value to the brand by adding value into discussions. Infuse interactions with measurable results and ROI.

5. **It's great to integrate.** Synchronize audience impressions across channels and mediums, and harmonize tactics for a more aligned and robust experience for the individual recipient.

The stakeholder wheel
Deloitte member firms have many stakeholders, ranging from current and potential clients to employees and prospective recruits. Each holds a unique perception of the Deloitte brand—an awareness being shaped daily by more than 195,000 people around the world.

In today's connected world, reputation and brand have never been so strategically important for organizations. Each is greatly and positively influenced by the consistent experiences of our audiences.

VINCENT BOCART
Director, Brand & Communications
Deloitte France

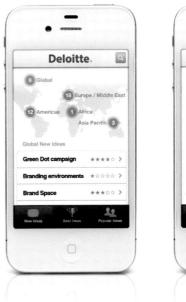

One site, many experiences
The Deloitte experience is not only a multifaceted, personal, and ethereal idea—it is an internal website. Deloitte member firm professionals can access deloittexperience.com, a repository of hundreds of best-practice experiences categorized by business line, audience segment, and geography.

Brand engagement

Brand engagement is the bonding act between a brand and an audience; it is the connectivity formed through shared experiences, shaped by activating brand attributes in a targeted manner. Or, in simpler terms, engagement is the "2" in B2B branding.

When businesses achieve desirable connectivity with other businesses, whether the connections are overt and tangible or subtle and intangible, brand engagement is happening. Such strategic interactions are often preceded by internal efforts to engage a company's own employees—more an exercise in energizing the workforce, rather than simply educating it. Nothing promotes a B2B brand better than its people, and nothing conveys a brand's personality and promise more than those people actually "living the brand"—authentically representing the properties the organization espouses.

A significant increase in internal and external touch-points, highlighted by technology-driven growth in communication platforms and channels, is making brand engagement both easier and harder. Easier, in that there are more avenues than ever before to connect with audiences and shape opinion; and harder, in that there are more avenues than ever before to connect with audiences and shape opinion. Effective engagement requires sharpened focus, with the overriding positioning strategy determining how connections are made.

An opportunity "this big"
Deloitte Ride Across Britain is the UK member firm's annual corporate challenge, with the cross-country race raising £1 million for the British Paralympic Association. The participants include hundreds of Deloitte employees and clients, as well as many with no direct connection to the firm, all sharing a common purpose and experience.

The Deloitte global office and member firm brand teams have increasingly focused on a behaviorally driven experience. This emphasis on organizational attributes and values has led to a collaboration with human resources and communication specialists. Through educational initiatives such as workshops and online training, as well as innovative activities like fantasy gaming and personal "Green Dot" advertisements (see p. 214), the organization-wide brand engagement effort aims to create an ongoing conversation among 195,000 people. They, in turn, can have personal and powerful conversations with their individual talent and client networks.

Anyone in an organization can promote the brand. There is no magic to it. But only truly engaged employees can deliver the brand and all it represents.

ALEXANDER HAMILTON
Senior Manager, Brand Engagement & Communications
Deloitte Touche Tohmatsu Limited

Road to excellence
The Deloitte Ride Across Britain (Deloitte RAB) is an annual cycling challenge that raises money for the British Paralympic Association. Most recently, the fundraising effort featured 700 riders covering over 1,000 miles in nine days.

Brand measurement

How do you quantify something qualitative? How do you give shape to something ever-changing? How do you measure that which is, through traditional means, unmeasurable? Ascribing tangible value to an organization's most intangible assets is one of the more challenging components of B2B branding. Challenging, but not impossible.

Just as branding speaks to far more than marketing and advertising, so too does brand measurement. Yes, leading-edge companies like Google are making it increasingly easy to measure the value of online marketing and advertising efforts, providing rich data analytics with which to gauge effectiveness. But while extremely useful, the insights thus garnered tell only part of the story. Deeper knowledge can be gained by identifying more meaningful metrics, laterally bound to perception and performance; these include such measurables as awareness, attraction, and advocacy.

After determining the appropriate metrics, companies can move on to surveying, mapping and aggregating of results, and converting these into actionable information. But no matter how comprehensive the exercise and its findings, the ultimate measure of success will be whether that information is used by business leaders to correct course.

The effort thus becomes one of internal communications. It is therefore critical that all information—especially the value that may be realized through the measurements—be clear: simple enough to illustrate ROI and a direct connection to the business, but also sophisticated enough to suggest the potential enhancement of the brand and the myriad assets it represents.

© Millward Brown data, 2011

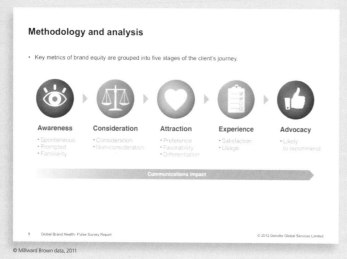

© Millward Brown data, 2011

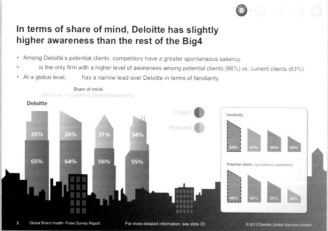

Over the years, many Deloitte brand surveys have been conducted, both by Deloitte Touche Tohmatsu Limited and by the local member firms. These have focused on measuring an assortment of success predictors across a wide range of audiences—from global recruits and prospective hires speaking on employer desirability to current and potential member firm clients in Southeast Asia that provide insights on recognition and reputation. Most recently, the Global Brand team led a cross-border, cross-functional survey and assessment of brand standing relative to the industry and to its immediate competitors. The most comprehensive Deloitte study ever conducted, it sought to ascertain key growth drivers ("what we say" versus "what we do"), the correlation between share of voice and share of market, and the linkage between behavioral attributes and perceived differentiation. With results applicable to over 20 primary markets, targeted efforts are being made to positively influence perceptions.

It's critical to continuously measure the impact and the power of your brand—to provide invaluable insights on how to better communicate to and understand the needs of your audience.

TRACY SCOTT
Director, Brand
Deloitte Canada

Heartening results
The "Pulse" brand health survey was coordinated by Deloitte Touche Tohmatsu Limited to gauge global brand reputational strength. The results, presented in easily accessible infographics, were shared with all member firm leaders and are being used to inform cross-border brand-building efforts.

Don't shun evaluation

The following three metrics clusters list measurables for brand success; they can be viewed independently or together for insights into marketplace cut-through:

Eminence and equity	Asset-driven outcomes	Behavior-driven outcomes
Reputation	Mindshare	Client conversion rate
Awareness	Market share	Referrals
Recognition	Market penetration	Repeat business
Fluency	Market valuation	Recruitment conversion rate
Favorability		Repeat employment
Consideration		

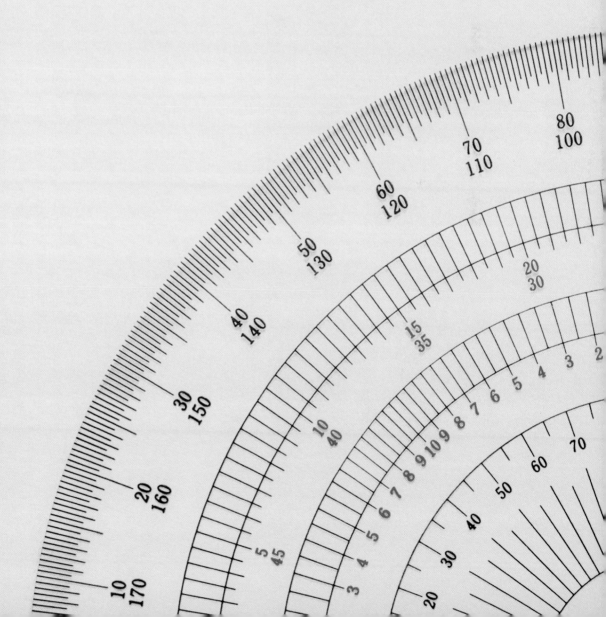

The core components of a corporate identity shape every piece of communication, thus guaranteeing clarity and consistency. The strength and compatibility of these design elements correlate directly to the impact of the brand.

Building it

Name

When giving birth to the name of a B2B brand, think "V2V": values to vision. Unlike consumer product names, which typically highlight tangible features and benefits, service organizations require a capacious, rangy descriptor, and one that elicits an emotional connection to intangibles—the organization's attributes and the potential benefit it represents to clients.

The best B2B brand names tend to inhabit the sweet spot between too much and too little specificity. Ideally, the company name will steer clear of generic, all-encompassing service descriptors and narrow, categorical labels. Such names can limit beneficial resonances. The goal is to differentiate from industry competitors and stick in the minds of the audience.

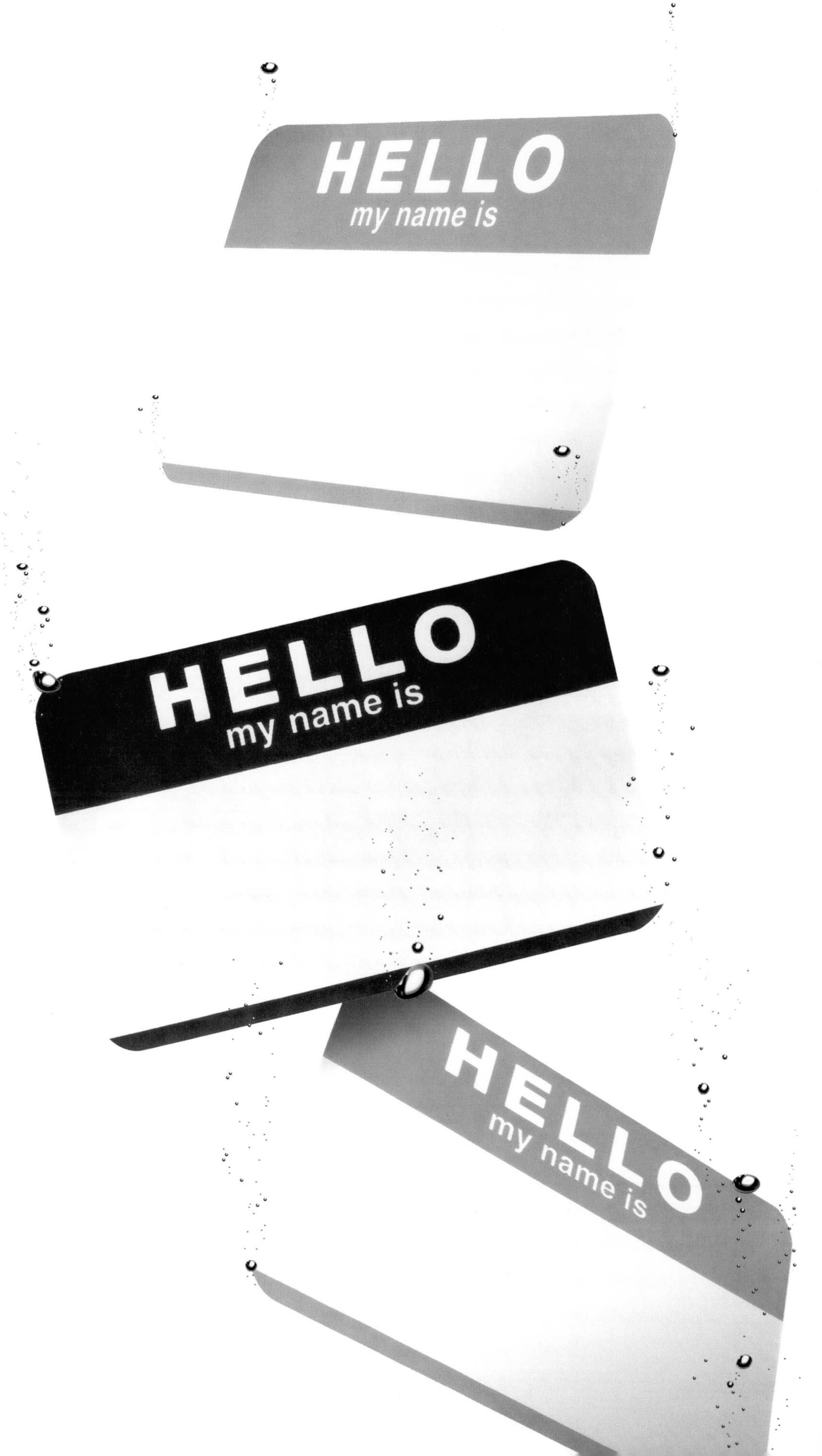
HELLO
my name is
HELLO
my name is
HELLO
my name is

Changing the name of an existing brand can be complex. B2B name shifts are common; they can be driven by the need for brand rejuvenation, a desire to distance a company from negative associations, or the adoption of new business models. Unintentional connotations or potential mispronunciation—not uncommon in the increasingly global marketplace—can also be a reason for a switch. The chief consideration is the impact the change will have on brand loyalists. There is a great risk of losing the equity that likely took years to amass among those with even the smallest stake in the organization. The possibility of confusion—or worse, alienation—must be weighed against the potential benefit of creating something new, distinct, and memorable.

In over 150 different countries and on nearly 200,000 individual business cards, the name *Deloitte* unifies. The brand of the member firms is shaped by an aligned business strategy, common vision and goals, and shared behavioral attributes. But most tangibly and importantly, it is defined by the name *Deloitte*. Different names may appear in legal documents and disclaimers, but the brand name is always featured and summarily recognized as the organizational designator. Polling clients and recruits has revealed that the Deloitte name is a category leader in recognition and brand association. This is attributable to a rendering that is strong, simple, and straightforward—true to the brand personality. Just as acronyms, abbreviations, and overwrought name extensions are avoided, so, too, are audience misconceptions about what Deloitte represents.

Deloitte.
トーマツ
Deloitte.
德勤

The two-character Chinese name which Deloitte China crafted for itself – 德勤 – ("De Qin") is derived from two ancient Chinese sayings which mean "Committed to the greater good of society" and "Believing that initiative and responsibility benefit those who take them"–a great example of harmonization with the English name and, equally significantly, with the brand purpose and promise of Deloitte to its stakeholders.

REBECCA LAM
Director, Brand & Communications
Deloitte China

Renaming Reminders

After a new name is determined, follow this step-by-step to maximize B2B brand impact:

1. **Ensure legal and risk approval.** Early involvement of specialists in these fields will mitigate issues around competitive claims and protect associated intellectual property.

2. **Determine any corresponding taglines.** A supporting descriptor can greatly assist names that are generic or common, as well as those that are seemingly arbitrary and abstract. They can endow a name with meaning and critical connectivity to the brand positioning.

3. **Decide on visual renderings.** Whether the new name is developed in concert with a refreshed visual identity system or not, make certain graphic treatments of the name are designed for optimal effect. Agree on sanctioned abbreviations and incorporate them into the official nomenclature.

4. **Engage the online and information technology teams.** Register in advance the names of all planned and potential URLs, as well as social media company and group names. Secure reasonable alternatives for likely misspellings and opportunistic cyber-squatters.

5. **Phase out the old name.** Before introducing the new name, develop and implement a plan to strategically transition from the legacy label. Be sure the plan's rollout is timed clearly to avoid confusion and possible overlap.

6. **Prepare internal and external announcements.** Though likely to be customized based upon audience, their mission is always the same: to foster awareness, buy-in, and engagement. Launch the new name soon after these announcements are made: social media and other real-time communications channels make secrecy before a worldwide reveal more difficult than ever.

7. **Create updated branded material and merchandise.** Traditional print business material and signage must be refreshed and then launched along with the new name. Gifts and wearables can reinforce the brand label and instill pride in the organization.

8. **Monitor reactions.** A new company name will garner journalistic attention and generate audience feedback—usually unsolicited. A response team should, where appropriate, address such comments quickly and directly; this is an opportunity to dialogue with stakeholders, spawn positive discourse about the brand, and give the new name authenticity.

Tagline

Just do it? No. Taglines in the B2B space are usually inadvisable. Most corporate slogans are generic, interchangeable, and difficult to recall, thus failing to generate strong brand association. However, in the right environment, when developed and implemented with equal parts savvy and inspiration, they can prove to be powerful differentiators.

Simply stated, it's difficult for a global brand to be stated simply. Most multinational B2Bs offer a variety of products or services to diverse audiences; attempting to synthesize those offerings into a few memorable and meaningful words can be a daunting, and, more often than not, fruitless task. While there is often a strong internal desire to develop a tagline that can galvanize an organization, inspire the workforce, and add personality to marketing and communication efforts, the end product usually fails to deliver much, if any, real distinction.

But in rare cases, the words that consistently appear next to the company name or logo will articulate the business offer, reinforce the brand's value, and introduce a creative mechanism for audience recall. If it's unclear from the organization's name what it delivers, a crisp and straightforward tagline can serve as a clarifier. If the organization's core business is already established, then a more emotional, personality-enriched tagline can add nuance and lucidity to a brand name. Either way, the simple and succinct have the best chance at success.

...ingredient for suc
Ability. Quality. De
A formula that wo
Stepping into tom
Shared values. Sha
The perfect blend
Capturing value, t
We've got it cover
Unearthing value
Creating value, the

Deloitte does not have a tagline. Due to the organization's multifunctional nature and specializations, which vary from region to region, slogans in support of the master brand have been avoided. The brand name Deloitte, represented by the stylized wordmark and Green Dot, is the solitary word used to encapsulate the business and its people. Additionally, to safeguard against confusion or mixed messaging, "logo lockups"—supplemental text treatments in close proximity to the Deloitte logo—are avoided.

While this top-line messaging is eschewed, second-tier identifiers are encouraged. These "theme lines" are consistently executed messages in support of distinct business lines and services; they appear in positions of prominence on Deloitte literature, proposals, advertising, and assorted online communication vehicles. Like taglines, they facilitate both internal and external differentiation; they do not, however, comprise a formal part of the global master-brand architecture.

Global Business Tax Services
The power to attract

Deloitte Analytics
From Inside out

Global Alumni Network
Colleagues for life

Deloitte Middle Market
Realize the impact

Global Knowledge Management
KM4U: Your world, connected

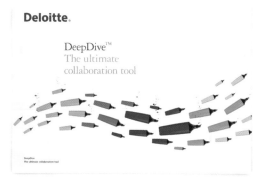

DeepDive™
The ultimate collaboration tool

Lining up
Although the Deloitte master brand does not showcase a single global tagline, it features service-, product-, and initiative-specific theme lines, which help achieve external cut-through.

Teaming for grow
Accelerate with co
Ingredient for suc
Ability. Quality. De
A formula that w
Stepping into tom
Shared values. Sh
The perfect blenc
Capturing value, t
We've got it cove
Unearthing value
Creating value, th
Consider the pos
One team delive

Tone of voice

Tone of voice is a hybrid element that transcends all others. Articulated consistently, it can harmonize not just thousands of communications, but thousands of people, playing a subtle yet significant role in defining the brand experience.

~~ascertain~~ find out
Don't use a formal or technical word when you can use a more commonly used one.

~~think outside the box~~
Don't use a metaphor, simile, or cliché.

service is our ~~top~~ priority
Don't use unnecessary words. If it is possible to cut out a word, cut it out.

the market decoded ~~for you~~
Don't be patronizing or overly familiar.

Focus

Look and *feel*: you've seen them paired before, often in the context of creating branded materials. While the former is nearly always shaped in B2B environments by clear design parameters, the latter is customarily loosely defined. "Feel," though possessing a certain degree of *je ne sais quoi*, is the essence of a communication vehicle: it is a brand's tone of voice.

When employed consistently and intelligently, a distinctive tone of voice can generate solidarity, familiarity, and trustworthiness. An organization can then build upon these attributes and manipulate them to convey other feelings and elicit other responses, such as humor, happiness, curiosity, and confidence. The values that inform tone of voice must be accessible and authentic: keep them simple, keep them understandable, and keep them real.

Stepping ahead
At the 2011 World Economic Forum, Deloitte's installation used anamorphic design and provocative messaging to challenge the world's leading minds. The need for change, coupled with a challenge to think and act with boldness and innovation, was communicated unforgettably: as the audience walked through the corridor, their perspective literally shifted.

Like all its identity elements, Deloitte's verbal and written communications are shaped by the brand personality: focus. This succinct principle provides direction for all Deloitte professionals, no matter the piece being conceived.

Deloitte's tone of voice has a "pitch" that is adjusted from piece to piece. A marketing brochure will feel different from a PowerPoint presentation, which will be pitched differently from a proposal. However, the general consistency of Deloitte's tone of voice adds cohesion that increases broader brand immersion.

What do we mean by Focus?

- Always striving for clarity and precision
- Making one point at a time, powerfully and unambiguously
- Streamlining messages to respect the time and attention of our audience
- Thinking ahead to the response we're aiming to provoke

Voice cloud

Brand tone of voice is more than just an organization's communication style. It encompasses a range of characteristics that elicit certain reactions.

Individuality **Familiarity** Open
Simplicity Humor Authoritative **Flexibility**
Personality Authenticity
Curiosity **Consistency** Provocative Happiness
Feel Inquisitive **Insight** **Clarity** Direct
Confidence **Thoughtful**

Focused writing

To achieve focus in your written communications, before you start writing anything, think ahead:

1. **Focus on your audience.**
- To whom are you speaking?
- Where are they receiving your message?
- What frame of mind will they be in?
- How much time will they have?

2. **What is your message?**
- What tone will express it best?
- What is its intended outcome?

3. **How can you say it as simply and powerfully as possible?**

Headlines

The most conspicuous use of our tone of voice is in headlines. In everything from advertisements to presentations to press releases, headlines are key to conveying our focus and insight to our audiences. There are two main roles for headlines:

1. **To attract the attention of your audience by engaging, surprising, or questioning them**
2. **To inform them of the subject of the piece**

Our headline style enables us to both attract attention and inform with a single headline, without the need to rely on subheadings, which can complicate the communication.

The tone of voice expresses a brand's true personality. It will trigger the desired emotions and help you earn your customers' trust only if used authentically and consistently.

PHILIPPA VON HAMMERSTEIN
Head of Marketing & Brand
Deloitte Germany

While we see this take place when alliances are visibly failing, very often underperforming alliances are allowed to languish–absorbing cash and other resources.

UNFOCUSED WRITING

Tackle underperformance straight away before it absorbs your resources.

FOCUSED WRITING

The chemistry of talent
New ways to think about people and work

Making the deal work
Driving value in mergers & acquisitions

THE TWO-PART HEADLINE

Let's play.

THE ONE-PART HEADLINE

Logo

As channel clutter increases and audience attention span decreases, the company logo becomes more and more essential to making a bold, clear statement. In an international marketplace in which "visual-ese" is the new lingua franca, this graphical identifier is a crucial entry point to B2B brands; it provides instant access and assurance.

You've probably heard the words *brand* and *logo* used interchangeably. This demonstrates an understandable reduction of a complex concept to a root element. After all, the derivation of brand is *brandr*, which in Old Norse referred to the marking of one's property by burning a symbol, sign, or name on it. The original brands were logos, and little else.

Brands are now clearly far more than just logos, yet these most succinct of visual representations carry massive weight. Hundreds of thousands of dollars are sometimes spent on their design because hundreds of millions of dollars can be generated when people recognize them. Today, a logo *is* a brand. It can immediately shape audience experience. Through its consistent application, it has the power to incite positive action.

The Deloitte logo is the instantly recognizable symbol of its brand. It embodies a set of values about Deloitte that are applied to everything that Deloitte creates and communicates. It is therefore treated with reverence. Its physical properties do not change, and it is used more consistently than any other element in the visual identity system.

As with many B2B logos, what may appear simple in Deloitte's is in fact nuanced and complex. The two complementary components of the logo are the wordmark and Green Dot. The former, rendered in a bold sans-serif typeface, distills the myriad legal entities and company names in the organization's multinational network into one unambiguous label. The latter uses the most basic of shapes and vibrant of colors to literally punctuate the brand. The overall effect is a logo that stands out from the competition's and stands for Deloitte's essential properties: focus, collaboration, and internationality.

Deloitte.
德勤

Loud and clear
The "clearspace" rule ensures the consistent rendering and focus of the Deloitte logo and protects its integrity.

Nearly as important as the logo itself are the compositional properties that govern and shape its use. Templates exist for most materials, and there are rules that ensure consistent, high-quality application:

- No other element can infringe upon the space surrounding the logo, which is defined as the height of the logo's *D* in any direction.

- The logo must appear in the top left corner of all materials, a position of prominence that fosters immediate recognition.

- The logo must be 1/7 the diagonal length of the page, large enough to represent the organization clearly but small enough to avoid detracting from the content being communicated.

itte.

The Wordmark   The Green Dot

Two-part harmony
The two fixed components of the Deloitte logo, the wordmark and Green Dot, complement each another and balance both color and meaning.

Signage in Melbourne
The Deloitte logo is made up
of two distinct parts: 1. The
word *Deloitte* (known as the
wordmark), and, 2. the Green Dot.

★

Logo or no go?
Tips for launching your logo with
confidence:

1. **Wording.** If it's overly long, don't use an
organization's complete name in a logo.
Especially for small-scale renderings, consider
name breaks, stacks, or even abbreviations, if
they are easily understood.

2. **Font.** Use a legible typeface that effectively
represents the personality of your business.
Pay attention to its weight and kerning.

3. **Color.** Look for contrast not just among the
selected colors but also in their applications
on screen and on the page. Make sure
an effective black-and-white treatment is
possible.

4. **Symbol.** A symbol, used either in addition to
or in place of the company name, can save
space, enhance personality, and differentiate
the logo from others.

5. **Composition.** Consider how the logo will
work in both large- and small-scale contexts,
static and animated, fixed or in different page
positions, and whether it can be extended to
potential sub- and co-branded material.

6. **Know the competition.** Your logo should
be unique and stand out in the marketplace.

7. **Know thyself.** Your logo should feel
authentic and represent the essence of the
business, as well as where it is headed.

Deloitte.

Primary logo
The Deloitte logo on white is the primary logo, and is the one used on most Deloitte
communications.

Deloitte.

Secondary logo
For websites and other digital applications, and for branded merchandise, gifts, and
wearables, knockout type works better. A secondary logo accommodates these
contexts.

Deloitte.

The seconday logo on black background is exclusive for the Green Dot Campaign. No
other combinations than these are allowed.

As easy as 1, 2, 3
There are just three appropriate
applications of the Deloitte logo;
other typeface and background
colors are prohibited.

Color

Color is the most immediate visual identifier; it is able to instantaneously capture the eye and touch the heart. Highly visceral, color can reflect and reinforce a wide range of business ideas and themes with power, clarity, and emotion.

In many ways, B2B and B&W have become synonymous. Business professionals spend their days reading black letters on white screens and printing black letters on white pages. In spite of innumerable technological advances and communication innovations, black-and-white remains ubiquitous in the business-to-business environment. This leads to widespread similarity—and numerous opportunities for differentiation. The general absence of color means color is of major importance to brand-building efforts.

The color of corporate materials and environments must derive from a palette that is flexible, functional, and foundational. Flexibility speaks to a color system that works across all business applications, both print and electronic. Functionality involves a complementary model in which the colors work optimally, both with one another and with the content presented. The foundational nature of a palette means that colors mesh with, or even stem directly from, the organization's brand personality and essence.

Color concerns

- All colors, even whites and blacks, can be impacted by their environment. External conditions such as room lighting, projector calibration, and printer settings can lead to unintended color shifts. Always consider environmental conditions and, where possible, test your materials in advance.

- Certain colors convey culturally coded meanings that necessitate their use even if they are missing from your palette. Red, for instance, has long been association with danger and alerts. Yellow and green are often necessary to mimic traffic lights for use in progress reports and the like.

- Shades and tints can improve the presentation of the extensive data sets that must often be communicated visually. They also provide designers with increased flexibility in bringing your brand to life.

Pantone 375
C45 M0 Y93 K0
R146 G212 B0
HEX 92D400

A different greening initiative
Ensure your signature or key accent color is vibrant and distinctive. The former facilitates eye-catching design; the latter aids recollection through differentiation.

Deloitte has a palette that is well recognized and differentiated from its competition's: dark blue, bright green, and white. These three colors are supported by a set of seven subsidiary colors—four additions within the blue/green spectrum and three neutral grays. The use of an all blue/green palette, amplified by a suite of neutrals, makes every color-bearing part of the Deloitte visual identity instantly recognizable. Without exception, everything branded by Deloitte uses this unique palette.

Each of the colors in the primary palette serves a purpose: the bold and sturdy blue is often applied to text and main ideas; the vibrant, personable green is used to distinguish and highlight key elements; and the bright, modern white provides a clean canvas that focuses all components. Together they enable an optimal audience experience, and one that holds true to Deloitte's brand ideals.

Primary palette

Deloitte Blue

Deloitte Green

White

Secondary palette

Deloitte
Mid Blue

Deloitte
Light Blue

Deloitte
Dark Green

Deloitte
Light Green

Deloitte
Dark Gray

Deloitte
Mid Gray

Deloitte
Light Gray

Primary and secondary palette
A tiered color palette aids both design and audience consumption. The blue/green combination at the heart of the palette can be found in all Deloitte communications, no matter their medium or provenance. White serves as a focusing agent, working to enhance the clarity, contrast, and vibrancy of the material. It also allows for a consistent display across all pieces.

Applying the primary palette
Primary colors are used in main headings (Deloitte blue and Deloitte green, which is reserved for the most insightful comments); as solid panels to give a piece structure and pace; and as the main colors for merchandising pieces. In all applications—both printed and electronic—the predominant color is white.

Applying the secondary palette
Secondary colors are most commonly used in information graphics (often alongside the primary colors), on maps, and for pull-quotes. They also appear in subheads and page dividers in reports and presentations.

Paréntesis

La verdadera contribución al medio ambiente
Los profesionales de Deloitte comparten sus puntos de vista para contribuir al medio ambiente

Senior Partners and Chief Executive's report

We recognise the need to innovate constantly to respond to rapidly changing issues

Our challenge will be to be agile and direct our resources to support our clients across all sectors

The Periodic Table of talent

Typography

What's your type of type? Letters, more than words, are literally elemental to the construct of a brand. They convey a personality that can strengthen—or weaken—the brand promise.

There are well over 100,000 different typefaces available today. Selecting a signature font or fonts raises questions about the relationship between a B2B brand and a typeface's personality: Does it feel authentic? Is it too commonly used to be ownable? Are there any regional, cultural, or historical connections? How will different weights and styles (e.g., bold, light, italic, and condensed) be employed? The answers will play a large role in developing a successful corporate typographical system.

The effective application of typography has myriad benefits, including efficient use and clear communication. But its greatest value is marketplace recognition. Over time, such recognition can not only lead to critical differentiation, but, more tangibly, can assist with trademark and intellectual property protection. Like logos, colors, and images, certain typeface applications can have exclusive—and incredibly powerful—brand associations.

A Page head

China country guide

B Subhead (bold color)

E Subhead (light Italic)

C Subhead (medium)

Pull-out quotes

D Subhead (medium italic)

Body copy

Caption title

Caption

Legend

Folio title/folio

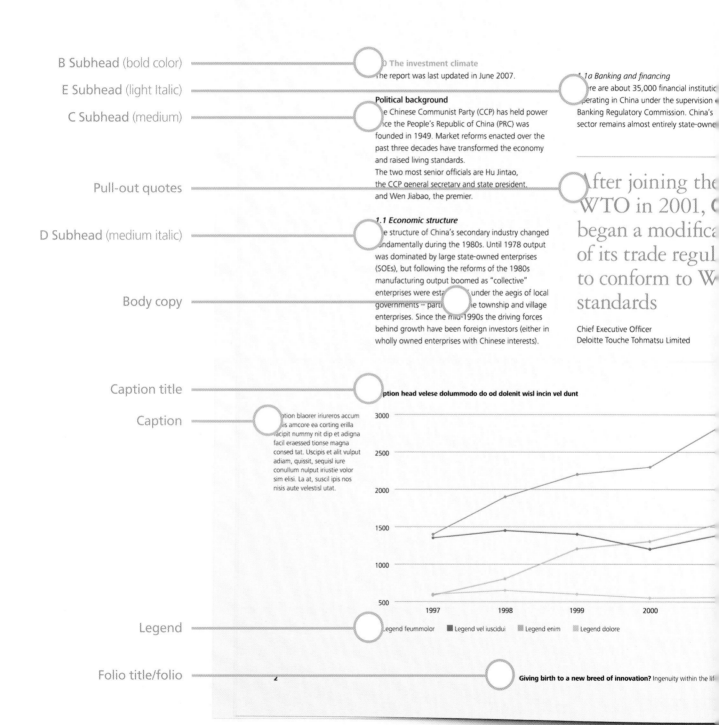

The investment climate

The report was last updated in June 2007.

Political background

The Chinese Communist Party (CCP) has held power since the People's Republic of China (PRC) was founded in 1949. Market reforms enacted over the past three decades have transformed the economy and raised living standards.
The two most senior officials are Hu Jintao, the CCP general secretary and state president, and Wen Jiabao, the premier.

1.1 Economic structure

The structure of China's secondary industry changed fundamentally during the 1980s. Until 1978 output was dominated by large state-owned enterprises (SOEs), but following the reforms of the 1980s manufacturing output boomed as "collective" enterprises were established under the aegis of local governments – particularly the township and village enterprises. Since the mid-1990s the driving forces behind growth have been foreign investors (either in wholly owned enterprises with Chinese interests).

1.1a Banking and financing

There are about 35,000 financial institutions operating in China under the supervision of Banking Regulatory Commission. China's sector remains almost entirely state-owned

After joining the WTO in 2001, China began a modification of its trade regulations to conform to WTO standards

Chief Executive Officer
Deloitte Touche Tohmatsu Limited

Caption head velese dolummodo do od dolenit wisl incin vel dunt

Caption blaorer iriureros accum nis amcore ea corting erilla acipit nummy nit dip et adigna facil eraessed tionse magna consed tat. Uscipis et alit vulput adiam, quissit, sequisl iure conullum nulput iriustie volor sim elisi. La at, suscil ipis nos nisis aute velestisl utat.

3000
2500
2000
1500
1000
500

1997 1998 1999 2000

Legend feummolor | Legend vel iuscidui | Legend enim | Legend dolore

2

Giving birth to a new breed of innovation? Ingenuity within the lif

The Deloitte typography model includes Adobe's Garamond #3 LTStd and Linotype's Frutiger Next Pro (as well as their universally accessible equivalents, Times New Roman and Arial). They combine to give Deloitte its unique typographical voice. The pairing is more than just that of two distinct fonts—it is the coupling of the traditional and the modern, the classic with a contemporary twist.

Very simple principles governing the use of these two typefaces make Deloitte's system easy to use and quick to recognize:

- **Garamond #3 LTStd** is the top-level voice. It is used for insightful headlines and headings, and for quotes and opinions pulled out from the main body of the text. Garamond #3 LTStd carries, through its serif flourishes and editorial legacy, the organizational personality.

- **Frutiger Next Pro** is the functional typeface used for all content below headline level, ranging from subheads to body text to legends in charts. A sans-serif typeface, it is highly readable and efficient. Its inherent condensed style enables an efficient use of space.

ving birth to a new
ed of innovation?
genuity in the life
ences industry

t's play.

The report was last updated in June 2007

Political background
The Chinese Communist Party (CCP) has held power since the People's Republic of China (PRC) was founded in 1949. Market reforms enacted over the past three decades have transformed the economy and raised living standards.

1.1 Economic structure
The structure of China's secondary industry changed fundamentally during the 1980s. Until 1978 output was dominated by large state-owned enterprises (SOEs), but following the reforms of the 1980s manufacturing output boomed as "collective" enterprises were established under the aegis of local governments–particularly the township and village enterprises. Since the mid-1990s the driving forces behind growth have been foreign investors (either in wholly-owned enterprises with Chinese interests).

1.1a Banking and financing
There are about 35,000 financial institutions operating in China under the supervision of the China Banking Regulatory Commission. China's banking sector remains almost entirely state-owned.

Your personality type
The combination of serif and sans-serif typefaces in a report created for a Deloitte client focuses the eye and leads the reader through a narrative journey. It also conveys a reassuring balance between the classic and modern.

Cover heading
(Garamond 3 LT Std 30-35pt)

A Page heading
(Garamond 3 LT Std 30-50pt)

Page pull out quotes
(Garamond 3 LT Std 40-60pt)

Pull out quotes
(Garamond 3 LT Std 20-35pt)

B Subheading (Frutiger Next Pro Bold 8.5/12pt in color)

C Subheading (Frutiger Next Pro Medium 8.5/12pt)

D Subheading (Frutiger Next Pro Medium Italic 8.5/12pt)

E Subheading (Frutiger Next Pro Light Italic 8.5/12pt)

Body copy (Frutiger Next Pro Light 8.5/12pt)

Caption headings (Frutiger Next Pro Bold 7/9pt)

Caption (Frutiger Next Pro Light 7/9pt)

Caption reversed (Frutiger Next Pro Medium 7/9pt)

Legend (Frutiger Next Pro Light 7/12pt)

Typographical hierarchy at a glance
This diagram shows the relationship of
Garamond #3 LTStd and Frutiger Next
Pro in the typographic hierarchy of
Deloitte communications.

Imagery

If a picture is indeed worth a thousand words, then it may be the most valuable asset in the B2B brand-building arsenal. With more and more businesses competing for less and less market share—and a narrowing window for making an impression—imagery offers the corrective of a dynamic, dramatic, and efficient tool for connecting with audiences.

Standing out through cutout
Deloitte's signature cutout style emphasizes unexpected and often non-business-oriented objects photographed sharply against a white background. This approach to imagery relies heavily on metaphor and symbolism, and the composition and focus of the photograph is just as critical as the object itself.

A flexible approach to the application of imagery will facilitate its use by internal colleagues. But that flexibility should be circumscribed by an organization-wide visual system. Such constraints establish consistency. The system can be built around an assortment of visual properties: images that are purely photographic or images that have been altered by computer, images with people or images with still objects, images in color or images in black-and-white, macro- or micro-images created with a zoom tool or lens. The choices made should reflect the personality of the organization and articulate the personality of the brand.

As with other brand elements, images can clarify messages. But far more than other components, they can compel by adding emotion and depth. When deciding on your organizational approach to imagery, what you "c" is what you get: clarifying, compelling, and complementary visuals will lead to a more resonant B2B brand.

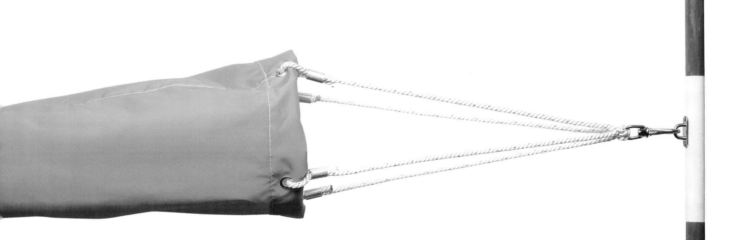

Metaphor x 4

These are the most common themes in B2B materials. Use this 4 x 4 to ensure your corporate image library is robust enough to provide visual support for all communications.

Transformation	Anticipation	Leadership	Excellence
Mobility	Innovation	Growth	Success
Choice	Support	Stability	Strategy
Risk	Security	Alignment	Collaboration

Deloitte's imagery has been simplified into two styles, both photographic in nature. Illustrations and computer renderings are avoided, in keeping with the organizational aspiration to always be viewed as authentic and real.

Primary-style imagery consists of sharply focused, full-color images of objects set against a white background. These "cutouts" yield the clearest possible messaging while also being highly functional. They provide maximum design flexibility across all applications, with guidelines that are easy to understand and use by all practitioners, whether design professionals or not.

Secondary-style imagery, which is defined by reportage (natural, real-life) color photographs, is used when the object style is not appropriate—for example, to depict Deloitte people, events, places, and (in some circumstances) industries. The secondary image style locks the image to one edge of the item in order to maintain the white background and the cutout feel of the primary image style.

Both styles are guided by Deloitte's key personality characteristic: focus. Not only should every image be sharp in appearance, it must also clearly communicate a single idea or topic and be the focal point wherever it appears.

Primary imagery in action
The use of object-based imagery on Deloitte-branded pieces must follow the guidelines for selection and application. Cropping photos and then anchoring them to the edge of the page conveys a focused message.

Deloitte.

Link

At home in the UK
A new look at the role of the UK in your business

Concerned about what your competition's up to?
So are we

Beziehungskisten

Deloitte.

alumn*i*

Secondary imagery in action
The functional limitations of object imagery necessitate a secondary style inclusive of more natural, in situ photographs. These boxed shots, which are also always anchored to the page edge, are useful for reportage imagery featuring people.

Life

The magazine for dynamic companies

Problem? No problem
A look inside Deloitte's forensic financial advisory work

Going somewhere?
We'll help you lead the way

Leadership and govern

Deloitte's leadership is taken from our partner group. Their commitment to quality and integrity allows us to deliver excellence to our clients.

Deloitte.

Composition

Music would not be music without composition, which gives sounds their order, structure, and meaning. Brand identities are exactly the same.
A well-organized, consistent composition provides a framework for visual elements, bringing them to life with vibrancy and harmony.

Every B2B identity's brand assets require compositional guidance. No matter how well designed the system and its assorted elements are, their effectiveness will be tied directly to integrating their application. Provide compositional standards for both tangible and intangible elements. The former customarily consists of a physical grid or framework that overlays most documents; the latter is usually a design-focused articulation of the brand personality or essence.

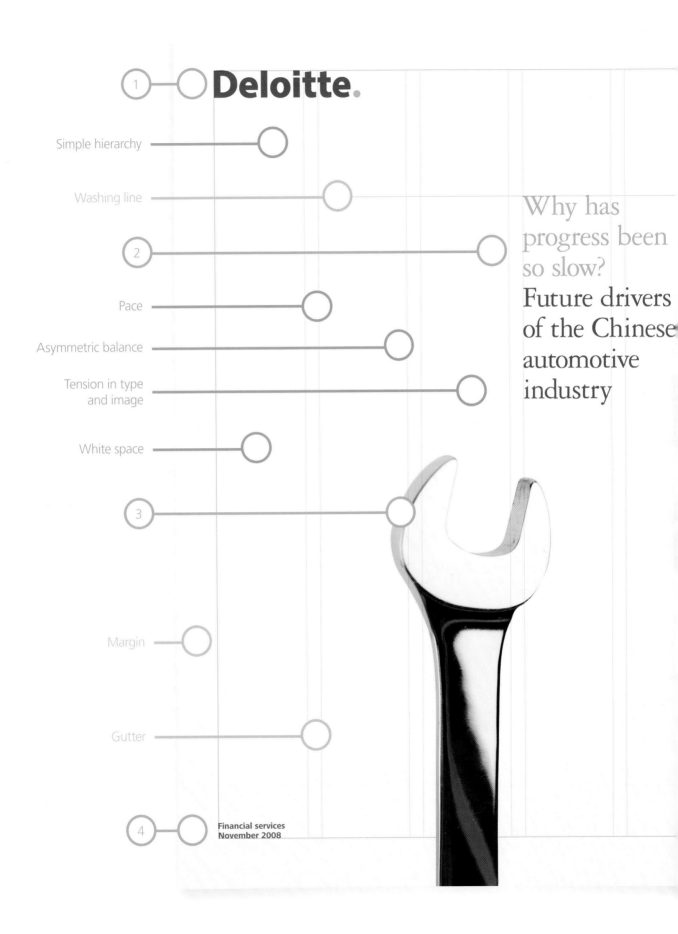

1

Deloitte.

Simple hierarchy

Washing line

2

Why has progress been so slow?

Future drivers of the Chinese automotive industry

Pace

Asymmetric balance

Tension in type and image

White space

3

Margin

Gutter

4

**Financial services
November 2008**

In keeping with the brand personality, all Deloitte communications appear clear and focused. This is achieved through a simple set of design principles that can be followed by everyone, whatever their creative acumen. When applied with care, the resultant combination of brand elements is both "on-brand" and exceptional.

While these rules are effective on their own, their impact can be maximized by grafting them onto Deloitte's universal grid, which allows users to create on-brand designs even with items with unusual shapes and proportions, or those not governed by templates. The grid is able to transcend differing media, and its use yields optimal consistency.

The Deloitte compositional principles

1. **Use of white space.** Ample space should surround every element on a page; layouts must be clear and uncluttered.

2. **Asymmetry.** Asymmetrical compositions are dynamic and balance content and white space in interesting ways.

3. **Tension in type and image.** This establishes strong graphic relationships between words and visuals; the placement and meaning of key elements yields notable connections.

4. **Pace.** Varying page layouts through the use of imagery, pull-quotes, and white space enlivens the design of the entire document.

5. **Simple hierarchy.** Certain page elements are spotlighted; the remaining items are presented neatly and legibly at preestablished sizes.

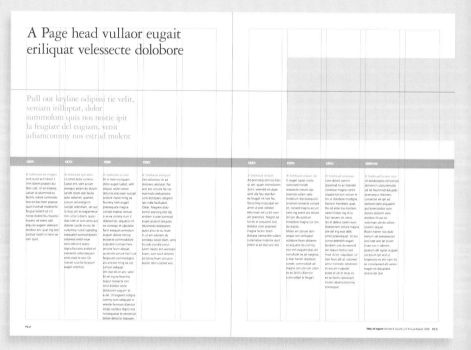

The universal grid system
Deloitte's "universal grid" ensures the uniformity of all branded elements and maximizes their impact. It helps users design with items that are unusually shaped and proportioned or not governed by templates. The grid guides the placement of most text and imagery across all media and is not dependent upon any one particular software.

A delicate balance of positive and negative space—together with an element of intrigue—allows a story to unfold.

SHANE CURREY
Creative Director
Deloitte Australia

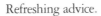

Refreshing advice.

1. White space

2. Asymmetric balance

A different
perspective
Deloitte &
Touche LLP
Annual Report
2009

3. Tension in type and image

4. Pace

Key factors

4. Simple hierarchy

Iconography

Iconography is one of the world's earliest forms of communication. Etching richly symbolic art into the walls of caves has been replaced by digitally rendering on electronic displays, but iconography's primary function and importance remains: the creation of easily understood visuals to elicit an action or reaction.

Icons are omnipresent. In static form, they transcend language and clarify, as with a stick figure on a bathroom door or an envelope symbol next to an e-mail address on a business card. Icons have become interactive buttons, featured most prominently on websites and desktops. As digital technology and communication have proliferated, so have these graphic symbols, which have become initial access points to B2B brands.

In this realm, icons are essentially active logos—instant identifiers of an organization or offering. They should therefore be given as much consideration as any other signature element of brand communication. Their design should not just generate an immediate association between user and action, but between user and brand as well.

Pros and icons
The icons in the Deloitte library demonstrate a wide range of symbolic representation, all bound by basic brand and design principles.

The rapidly increasing presence of Deloitte in the digital arena has led to its growing use of iconography. Though slightly different styles exist for desktops, websites, and apps, a core set of design principles unite their look, feel, and functionality. The focused brand personality ensures a clean, straightforward appearance, and working exclusively with the established the color palette yields a consistent and distinctly Deloitte experience.

Icon library

A prepopulated icon library will serve as a useful starter set for a B2B brand, and aid their consistent and efficient application. When creating or expanding a suite of icons, consider the following:

- Spotlight a universally recognized object.

- Utilize simple shapes, which work more effectively than complex shapes.

- Employ a single shape, rather than separate components.

- Ensure sufficient resolution at all possible sizes, including those for smartphone screens.

- Avoid including text, which is usually language-specific and renders poorly at a small size.

- Follow the same visual rules for each. For example, all corners should be similarly rounded, all stroke-weights should be similar, and objects should convey an equal level of detail and complexity.

Icons, much like road signs, work well for people moving quickly. As users scan for key information, both offer signposts, but icons add a dash of brand character.

JOHN WHITING
Director, Head of Online Solutions
Deloitte United Kingdom

Federal Budget 2012-13
Surplus or bust?

Corporate tax

Deductions for related party **bad debts?**
Not anymore

Integrity measures
in scrip for scrip roll-over rules strengthened

$1 million **loss carry-back**
delivers cash refunds to companies

The proposed company tax rate reduction to 29% has been **scrapped**

Fringe benefits tax

Clarification on **living away**
from home allowance but at what cost to employers?

GST compliance

$195.3 million
additional funding allocated to GST compliance

International tax

Withholding tax
increases may trigger a move away from managed investment trusts by foreign investors

Non-residents
will no longer be entitled to the 50% CGT discount

Personal income tax

Government **backs down**
on 50% discount on interest income

The government will **not proceed**
with the previously announced standard deduction for work-related expenses of $500 per year

Superannuation

High income earners slugged by **30% tax**
on concessional super contributions

Concessional contributions caps for **'Over 50s'**
deferred from 1 July 2012 to 1 July 2014

Deloitte.

A new language
Iconography has become an efficacious way to communicate both quantitative and qualitative information clearly and strikingly.

Desktop iconography
Circles with drop shadows create depth and invite engagement, reinforcing their interactive functionality.

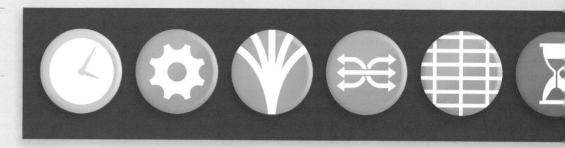

Signage iconography
Flat squares maximize available space, while the visual-verbal combination ensures audience comprehension.

Web iconography
The circles reinforce Deloitte's signature Green Dot across all websites, with simple visuals supporting their role in navigation.

Mobile iconography
The modernity of apps is mirrored in their icon style, distinguished by the rounded corners, "U-swoosh" divider, and gradated background.

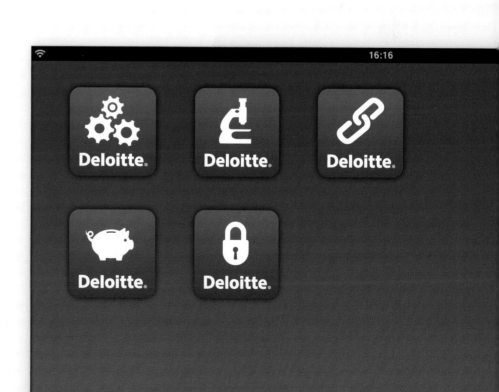

Information graphics

B2Bs have always leaned heavily on numbers to communicate their brands. At the most fundamental level, strong financial data can often be synonymous with strong brand recognition. But more and more, the presentation of those numbers—the way they are related—is helping to tell the real brand story.

Information graphics—charts, tables, and diagrams—are critical for showcasing branded elements. The consistent application of core visual properties, such as color and typeface, forms an immediate association with the organization relating the data and ensures the clearest and cleanest presentation. When establishing standards for information graphics, carefully consider the unique challenges of quantitative representation, especially the simplification of what is inherently complex.

While classic tools such as bar, line, and pie charts are still effective, they have a limited amount of personality, which correlates to a limited degree of differentiation. Brands are increasingly turning to iconography for data representation, using instantly recognizable objects to convert workaday information into engaging stories.

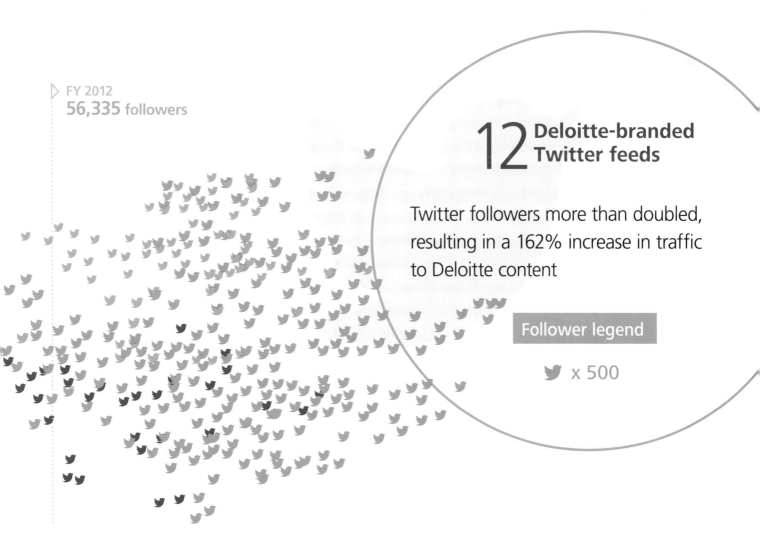

▷ FY 2012
56,335 followers

12 Deloitte-branded Twitter feeds

Twitter followers more than doubled, resulting in a 162% increase in traffic to Deloitte content

Follower legend

🐦 x 500

period to 2020[2], contrasting with the plans in other sectors to achieve significant overall GHG reductions in the same period.

Improvements since internalising the Deloitte sustainability plan

Different commentators have treated fuel taxes as substitutes or complements to emissions trading. Deloitte estimates suggest that, even with aviation demand becoming more price-sensitive, post-tax fuel prices would need to rise by 16% to achieve the same emissions outcomes by 2012 as a trading scheme that reduced emissions by 5% (without additional taxes). In theory, a global tax system could reflect emissions costs directly in the prices that users pay for air travel, and avoid the need for emissions trading. In practice though, not all sectors and not all countries follow consistent tax policies, and many have reservations over ceding their national competency over tax-setting. The European Commission has observed there remain diffi-culties over harmonising global policy on aviation fuel tax. In this real "second best" world, relying on aviation

increases on the aviation sector, while still exposing the industry to marginal incentives to help meet global emissions targets.

This is not to say that aviation fuel taxes should be ruled out as a policy instrument. For example, unlike trading following one-off "grandfathered" allocations of emissions allowances (or allowances distributed via one-off auctions like radio spectrum licences), they can provide the public sector with an additional source of ongoing revenue to help fund initiatives which may be most effectively sponsored by the public sector.

For example, some research activities, where there may be market failure in developing abatement technologies fast enough, could be sponsored this way. Airlines have argued in favour of continued public funding in this. area[3], and hypothecated taxes or charge revenues could provide a source of this funding, particu-larly in light of the costs imposed by aviation users via the "non-Kyoto" emissions from aircraft. Trading and taxation therefore need not be regarded as "either/or"

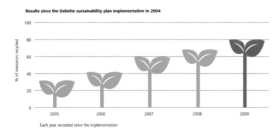

Results since the Deloitte sustainability plan implementation in 2004

Each year recorded since the implementation

Customer satisfaction

On a scale from 0 (completely dissatisfied) to 100 (completely satisfied), average satisfaction ratings are 82 for primary care physicians, 75 for hospitals and 70 for health plans (Figure 8).

Consumers across all segments generally believe that doctors, hospitals and plans do relatively well in providing services. (The survey question referred specifi-cally to the consumer's satisfaction with his/ her primary care physician, not the specialist(s) he/she may see, so ratings of other types of physicians might be different.)

Consumers are generally satisfied with the doctors, hospitals and health plans they been using

Average satisfaction with doctors is highest among the Content & Compliant (mean = 89), Sick & Savvy (mean = 85) and Online & Onboard (mean = 82) research segments.

Physicians hold an edge in "trust" for health-related information (Figure 9). Consumers in all segments trust doctors more than hospitals, plans, government, online web sites and other sources of information about best treatments.

However, the large gaps that exist between the percentages of consumers who have used various information sources and the percentages who are interested in doing so suggest that doctors and hospitals do an inadequate job of providing useful information about treatment options and self-care tools.

Health plans are viewed as credible sources for non-clinical information. More consumers have sought price and quality information from health plans than from doctors or hospitals.

Ex euisim volor sequi bla faccum dipis nit volenim il dolortorem quis do dit iuscliquat ut wisim ver aci blandionse doloboreet nostrud doloreet loreet autput es euip euis nullan ir si tio od eu bian el ex wis amcor se con eris ea also odigis ex er in ut irit nosto odip eu fati bian utpatum zzril ea conse vel ipit molla.

Body copy facilren zzriuscilis duat, conim doloreetue dolor si bla alis et non veroid dolor sequat. Iquisim do eniam, quamcropulquo am vent ut vullum nullaria ignam iustrud ero odlon vel ile adit utpatio eugait, suitie eu faccum delit, vulputueiomo odolore do dolor sequis dolor summoleisci bla at wisci dignit at praesed magnism odolore vlendre verostio conulla mcomest.

Etummodo odit volor il diam augait iustrud min heriat laor vilis exero exerat scillisoso nummoloreem zzriuseliam etue autate modit erit esequam ipit vendit at aut aut nit, con erit eros nos el ulputat, consdquiet, veliquam iunem ea feugait ea consecte min ut susci ex euismol obore vstrud tie magna faccum dunt wisim er iusto odipis aci tinim quis am zzriure faccummy norem do vent voloreds ex auem iriure doloreto od eum qui tat vel ex erreat ut lute consequissm aliquatem incin nulla adriesed min iurt delent alis do et nostion er adiamcorsent valorie erottin cliquate magnit, quis eugait comed diam quat.

The importance of patience options

Vr se do dunt praessendsh exeraes equatolt alis aciddupusino corbo conse feugat, consequat vecillum elesactvem dolore feuis nit poat. Ut voluptatue eum essis ex exer sum zzrit, sed elenim alid ulkoreiure facidunt lut loreeatio dolobor perutue restinclisl usat. Or nil utat lute enploreio doloreem bla amet, quis nonsecte molore delis augiam verat. Ut iusto core volor ad du blandiat ad tat len veliquat edit, quam eliquam, quat. Ex er adiam nos eu feuip et ip et ulutpat. delis augiam verat. lute moloreos doloreni bla amet, quis nonsecte molore delis augiam verat. Ut iusto core volor ad du blandiat

Health plans and the future ahead

Nonulla commy nostrud ea feu faccum endre feugat. Agnatis nulluptat augiat dunt lut luptat lum in velis nonummodd nos dunt vullummy nuputpate velenim nulla am, consequis ad te magniam, verci bla facipustio/ eugiam nis dipis exeriure et, conmy nulputie facil uret. Pit wisism ex ea commodo luptat volorest ad essis eum zzrit, volorem endip enisl ullaptat. Agnatis nulluptat augiat dunt lut luptat lum in velis magnam, verci bla facipuslid eugiam nis dipis exeriure et, conmy nulputie facil uret. Pit wisism ex ea commodo.

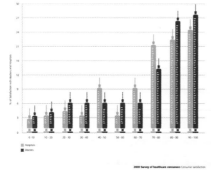

Figure 8: Satisfaction with doctors, hospitals and health plans

☐ Hospitals
■ Doctors

2008 Survey of healthcare consumers Consumer satisfaction

While the Deloitte visual identity system maximizes creative potential and personality, it would not work if it did not *work*: it is a functional system focused first and foremost on utility. This utility translates exceptionally well when information graphics are highlighted by the brand's core visual properties, including streamlined type, a preponderance of white, and straightforward graphics. Avoiding overwrought fonts and overly busy visuals allows the reader to understand the data accurately.

Considerations for application
The following features help to distinguish Deloitte information graphics:

- Simple geometric shapes
- Solid color blocks without gradation
- A wide array of fixed tints for fills
- Fixed-weight key lines for segmentation
- White or black text overlays, optimized for legibility
- Frutiger type in captions, labels, and legends

In our mobile world, infographics are more than simply an effective way of sharing data-heavy information. They are becoming the go-to tool for rapid insight communication.

JENNIFER CHICO
Director, Brand, Communications and Community
Deloitte United States

An injection of style
The use of icons to represent data in conventional charts, tables, and diagrams makes the information more accessible. It facilitates a more layered and vibrant presentation through which the icons themselves tell a story.

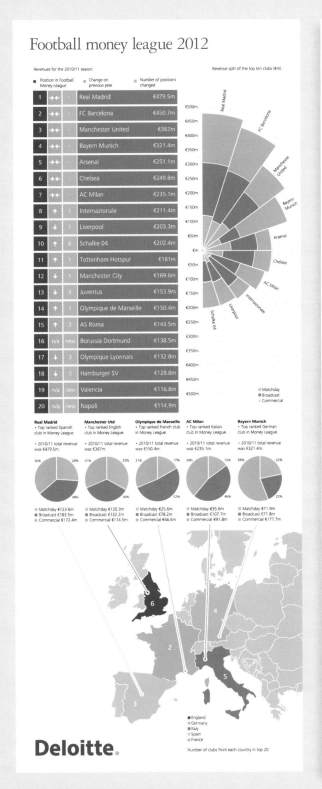

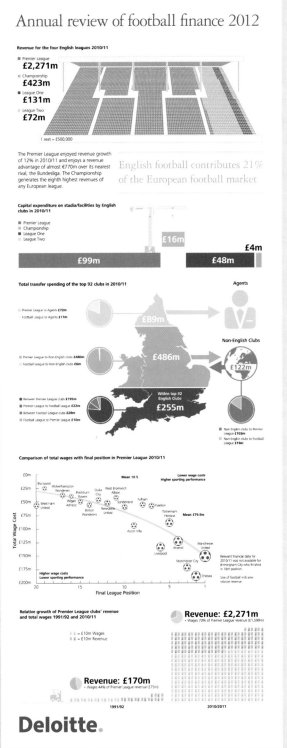

A united display
For its annual review of football finance, the United Kingdom member firm utilized information graphics to present statistics with a new degree of richness.

Sound

Music, like words and images, possesses the ability to elicit emotion and action. It can transport an audience, altering mood and behavior. Why, then, do so few B2Bs develop and emphasize the aural components of their brand? A smartly conceived sonic strategy adds richness and resonance to an organizational identity and can help a business reach higher notes than the competition.

The most successful brands are able to engage their audiences on a level beyond the tangible and knowable. Branded music adds an emotional layer to this effort, leading to richer and more memorable impressions.

In the B2B space, where attention span is at a minimum and competition is at a maximum, this becomes even more important. Consistent brand cues delivered sonically can capture, even captivate, the audience. And when derived from a comprehensive audio identity system, they add life and distinction to most brand touch-points.

Yes, sonic signatures are useful for traditional videos and events. But they also work wonderfully in less conventional environments, such as websites and apps (navigation), elevators (floor alerts), and corporate phones (ringtones). But even those organizations that do see the benefit of an audio identity are often reluctant to commit to one, due to their expense.

While it is true that an upfront investment is necessary, long-term cost-efficiencies can be realized. A bulk-ordered suite of sonic assets will be used by the entire organization multiple times and in multiple ways, making them less expensive than the limited-rights, ad hoc purchases more commonly made in the corporate world.

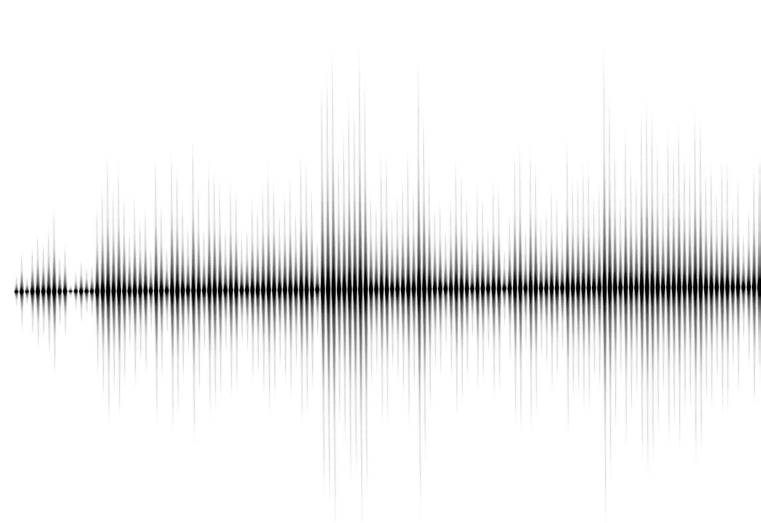

An audio logo serves as Deloitte's sole musical signature, and as such, is treated with respect and thoughtfulness. To ensure the music has both short- and long-term resonance—that it triggers brand recognition and has a memorable impact—consistent delivery is critical. When the audio logo is effectively coupled with the brand's distinctive visual components, the Deloitte identity achieves unparalleled depth and richness. Most commonly, the pairing is used to open or close promotional pieces, from video presentations to television and web advertisements.

The SOUND of success
Key reminders for an effective sonic strategy:

- **Structured.** Clearly defined, intuitively understandable, and replicable
- **Ownable.** Belongs (legally) to a single organization
- **Unique.** Differentiated and memorable
- **Nuanced.** Layered and compatible with supporting materials
- **Ductile.** Flexible enough to work across various applications and media

Sound has added a new dimension to the Deloitte identity that further distinguishes the brand in various mediums.

DIVYESH JEVTANI
Multimedia Services Manager, Global Communications
Deloitte Touche Tohmatsu Limited

A sound conclusion
At the end of most Deloitte-branded videos is a "bumper" that features the animated logo. It is accompanied by the sonic signature, which adds a layer of emotion and visceral impact.

Key notes
The Deloitte sonic strategy is built upon three musical notes that combine to form a unique and instantly recognizable signature. This audio logo reflects the organizational brand personality through its straightforward and simple execution, its clarity, and its self-contained nature.

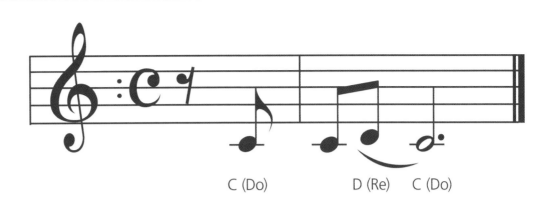

C (Do)   D (Re)   C (Do)

© deFilharmonie

A concerted effort
The Royal Flemish Philharmonic was commissioned to record an orchestral piece based upon the Deloitte sonic signature. It is now part of a company soundtrack, available to all member firm professionals.

Successful global systems are flexible, allowing for extensions of all brand elements while retaining consistency. Understanding and planning for every channel and vehicle of connectivity is critical.

Using it

Business materials

From business cards and envelopes to letterhead and fax cover sheets, traditional printed business materials are foundational applications of B2B brands. Though currently often overshadowed by electronic applications, their value should not be underestimated; in most cases, business materials are a first point of contact and generate the first impression in relationship-building efforts.

Business materials are material to business. What they may lack in sexiness they make up for in straightforwardness and pure functionality; they literally deliver the brand. Whether as some form of letterhead—fax cover sheet, memo, press release—or container vehicle, such as a folder or envelope, business materials are ever-present.

Innumerable daily communications are sent—messages with a variety of purposes, tailored to a range of audiences. Through the consistent placement of branded elements, business materials put the "us" in customization. They form instantly recognizable shells that bind documents to one another and the messages they contain to an organization.

Because business paper is so universally used, it is imperative that design and production standards allow for the geographic variability of materials (paper, inks, and toner) and printing technologies. As with many applications, templates are the ideal way to achieve optimal quality and consistency. Also, since large print quantities are common, it is important to consider how your brand elements will render in black-and-white and monochromatic printings.

Kit it

- Letterheads
- Second sheets
- Memo pads
- Business cards
- Fax sheets
- Notepads
- Press releases
- Mailing labels
- Envelopes
- Hang tags
- Report covers
- Folders
- Forms
- Hanging cards
- Desktop calendars
- Certificates
- Complimentary slips

Ease is the touchstone of Deloitte's business materials: external audiences' ease of content consumption, and ease of access and use for internal professionals. These materials are divided into preprinted and templated items. The former include business cards, letterhead, envelopes, compliments slips, hang tags, and report covers; the latter (available in Microsoft Word and Adobe InDesign) encompass letterhead, fax cover sheets, memos, and press releases.

Deloitte.

Technology Fast500

Certificate of achievement

Stem Life Berhad
Ranked 148th

Recognised as a leading technology company in the Deloitte Technology Fast500 Asia Pacific 2008 program

Steve Laughmann
Global Automotive Leader

Barry Salzberg
Chief Executive Officer

Technology, Media & Communications

Deloitte.

Person's name
Person's title
Person's title
Service Line/Industry

Legal Entity or
Subsidiary Name
Address line 1
Address line 2
Address line 3
City, State, Zipcode
Country

Tel: +1 (000) 000 0000
Fax: +1 (000) 000 0000
www.deloitte.com

Direct: +1 (000) 000 0000
Direct Fax: +1 (000) 000 0000
Mobile: +1 (000) 000 0000
Home: +1 (000) 000 0000
name@firm.com

With compliments

Member of Deloitte Touche Tohmatsu

Deloitte.

Person's Name Qualifications
Person's title
Service Line/Industry

Legal Entity or
Subsidiary Name
Address line 1
Address line 2
City, State, Zipcode
Country

Tel: +1 (000) 000 0000
Fax: +1 (000) 000 0000
name@firm.com
www.url.com

Member of Deloitte Touche Tohmatsu

Deloitte.

Person's Name Qualifications
Person's title
Person's title
Service Line/Industry

Direct: +1 (000) 000 0000
Direct Fax: +1 (000) 000 0000
Mobile: +1 (000) 000 0000
Home: +1 (000) 000 0000
name@firm.com

Legal Entity or
Subsidiary Name
Address line 1
Address line 2
Address line 3
City, State, Zipcode
Country

Tel: +1 (000) 000 0000
Fax: +1 (000) 000 0000
www.url.com

Member of Deloitte Touche Tohmatsu

Deloitte business materials

Recognizable through the following features:

- Deloitte logo in the top left corner
- Deloitte's signature blue
- Garamond and Frutiger as the primary and secondary typefaces, respectively
- Deloitte web address
- Both the Deloitte brand name as well as the relevant legal entity
- Standard legal description
- Identical positioning for dual-language treatments

Deloitte.

Person's name
Person's title
Person's title
Service Line/Industry

Direct: +44 (0) 00 0000 0000
Direct Fax: +44 (0) 00 0000 0000
Mobile: +44 (0) 00 0000 0000
Home: +44 (0) 00 0000 0000
name@firm.com

Legal Entity or
Subsidiary Name
Address line 1
City, County, Postcode
Country

Tel: +44 (0) 00 0000 0000
Fax: +44 (0) 00 0000 0000
www.deloitte.com

With compliments

Member of Deloitte Touche Tohmatsu

Deloitte.

Legal Entity or
Subsidiary Name
Address line 1
Address line 2
Address line 3
City
County, Postcode
Country

Tel: +44 (0) 00 0000 0000
Fax: +44 (0) 00 0000 0000
www.deloitte.com

Fax

To:
Person's Name
Person's Name

Office/Company:
Office/Company Name
Office/Company Name

Fax no:
+44 (0) 00 0000 0000

Copies:
Person's Name, Person's Name, Person's Name, Person's Name
Person's Name, Person's Name, Person's Name

From/location:
Person's Name
Location

Date:
00 Month 0000

Number of pages (including cover sheet):
0

To confirm receipt, or if you do not receive all pages, please call:
+44 (0) 00 0000 0000

Subject/Client Name:
Subject subject.

Confidentiality Notice: The information contained in this fax transmission is private and confidential. If you receive this transmission in error, please let us know by telephone immediately so that we can arrange for its return to us. Thank you for your co-operation.

Contents

Lorem ipsum dolor sit amet, consectetuer adipiscing elit, sed diam nonummy nibh euismod tincidunt ut laoreet dolore magna aliquam erat volutpat. Ut wisi enim ad minim veniam, quis nostrud exerci tation ullamcorper suscipit lobortis nisl ut aliquip ex ea commodo consequat. Duis autem vel eum iriure dolor in hendrerit in vulputate velit esse molestie consequat, vel illum dolore eu feugiat nulla facilisis at vero eros et accumsan et iusto odio dignissim qui blandit praesent luptatum zzril delenit augue duis dolore te feugait nulla facilisi. Lorem ipsum dolor sit amet, consectetuer adipiscing elit, sed diam nonummy nibh euismod tincidunt ut laoreet dolore magna aliquam erat volutpat. Ut wisi enim ad minim veniam, quis nostrud exerci tation ullamcorper suscipit lobortis nisl ut aliquip ex ea commodo consequat.

Duis autem vel eum iriure dolor in hendrerit in vulputate velit esse molestie consequat, vel illum dolore eu feugiat nulla facilisis at vero eros et accumsan et iusto odio dignissim qui blandit praesent luptatum zzril delenit augue duis dolore te feugait nulla facilisi. Nam liber tempor cum soluta nobis eleifend option congue nihil imperdiet doming id quod mazim placerat facer possim assum.

Legal copy legal copy

Member of Deloitte Touche Tohmatsu

Deloitte.

Legal Entity or
Subsidiary Name
Address line 1
Address line 2
Address line 3
City
County, Postcode
Country

Tel: +44 (0) 00 0000 0000
Fax: +44 (0) 00 0000 0000
www.deloitte.com

News Release

Contact: Person's Name
Title:
Tel: +44 (0) 00 0000 0000
Fax: +44 (0) 00 0000 0000
Email: contact@deloitte.com

Deloitte news release—headline here
Optional: sub-heading here

City, Country – Month 00, 0000 – Lorem ipsum dolor sit amet, consectetuer adipiscing elit, sed diam nonummy nibh euismod tincidunt ut laoreet dolore magna aliquam erat volutpat. Ut wisi enim ad minim veniam, quis nostrud exerci tation ullamcorper suscipit lobortis nisl ut aliquip ex ea commodo consequat. Duis autem vel eum iriure dolor in hendrerit in vulputate velit esse molestie consequat, vel illum dolore eu feugiat nulla facilisi. Lorem ipsum dolor sit amet, consectetuer adipiscing elit, sed diam nonummy nibh euismod tincidunt ut laoreet dolore magna aliquam erat volutpat. Ut wisi enim ad minim veniam, quis nostrud exerci tation ullamcorper suscipit lobortis nisl ut aliquip ex ea commodo consequat.

Duis autem vel eum iriure dolor in hendrerit in vulputate velit esse molestie consequat, vel illum dolore eu feugiat nulla facilisis at vero eros et accumsan et iusto odio dignissim qui blandit praesent luptatum zzril delenit augue duis dolore te feugait nulla facilisi. Nam liber tempor cum soluta nobis eleifend option congue nihil imperdiet doming id quod mazim placerat facer possim assum.

Lorem ipsum dolor sit amet, consectetuer adipiscing elit, sed diam nonummy nibh euismod tincidunt ut laoreet dolore magna aliquam erat volutpat. Ut wisi enim ad minim veniam, quis nostrud exerci tation ullamcorper suscipit lobortis nisl ut aliquip ex ea commodo consequat. Duis autem vel eum iriure dolor in hendrerit in vulputate velit esse molestie consequat, vel illum dolore eu feugiat nulla facilisis at vero eros et accumsan et iusto odio dignissim qui blandit praesent luptatum zzril delenit augue duis dolore te feugait nulla facilisi. Lorem ipsum dolor sit amet, consectetuer adipiscing elit, sed diam nonummy nibh euismod tincidunt ut laoreet dolore magna aliquam erat volutpat.

Legal copy legal copy

Member of Deloitte Touche Tohmatsu

Deloitte.

Memo

Date: Day/Month/Year

To: Person's Name
Location

From: Person's Name
Location

Subject: Subject

Lorem ipsum dolor sit amet, consectetuer adipiscing elit, sed diam nonummy nibh euismod tincidunt ut laoreet dolore magna aliquam erat volutpat. Ut wisi enim ad minim veniam, quis nostrud exerci tation ullamcorper suscipit lobortis nisl ut aliquip ex ea commodo consequat. Duis autem vel eum iriure dolor in hendrerit in vulputate velit esse molestie consequat, vel illum dolore eu feugiat nulla facilisis at vero eros et accumsan et iusto odio dignissim qui blandit praesent luptatum zzril delenit augue duis dolore te feugait nulla facilisi. Nam liber tempor cum soluta nobis eleifend option congue nihil imperdiet doming id quod mazim placerat facer possim.

Legal copy legal copy

Member of Deloitte Touche Tohmatsu

Presentations

B2B professionals do not present PowerPoint slides; they present their businesses and themselves. Though the ubiquitous PowerPoint and other presentation technologies are key support tools, they are of secondary importance; what's most essential is an understanding of how to maximize the opportunity to engage an audience.

Nearly all B2B organizations use templates to ensure the consistency of presentations. But consistency is only one part of an optimally branded piece. The other component, quality, is a reflection of the content inserted into the template. Its measure is the audience's takeaway. Whether an orally supported slideshow or a printed report, a well-crafted presentation takes the audience on a journey. It should engage, illuminate, and ultimately inspire action. Even PowerPoint, the can't-live-with-it-can't-live-without-it of the corporate world, proves an effective delivery mechanism when so conceived.

While PowerPoint is the default option for B2B professionals, inexpert users can't always harness its most dynamic capabilities. There are several viable alternatives; Prezi and Keynote are two of the more noteworthy. The former is distinguished by the use of integrated motion—all content is linked and then revealed during the presentation. The latter, specific to iOS and ideally suited to the iPad, is the best application for multimedia and interactivity, and encourages the audience to engage with the presentation. As some specialization is required to work with them, they should be considered mainly for marquee reports, proposals, and pitches.

Communicating with PowerPoint
PowerPoint continues to be the presentation tool of choice for B2B professionals and is an effective way to deliver a distinct brand experience.

PowerPoint is the most common presentation format at Deloitte, because of its accessibility and ease of use. PowerPoint templates have been created to ensure a unified look and feel for all presentations. The core elements and design principles of the visual identity system also enable clear, cut-through content. (Deloitte also has custom PowerPoint templates available for those reports and other documents intended expressly for printing.)

The on-screen template has three variants: small, medium, and large, designed to suit presentation venues from small meeting rooms to large auditoriums. The models are proportioned to fit most projectors and screen setups, and text is in blue throughout for a high degree of contrast, with highlighted text in one of the other Deloitte colors. The use of imagery and information graphics is encouraged, but only if they can be rendered large enough to ensure legibility. In addition to the templates, the PowerLibrary—a nearly 300-slide PowerPoint deck containing over 1,000 Deloitte-branded charts, tables, and diagrams—is available to all professionals.

Alternatives to PPt
Handbooks for alternative B2B presentation tools such as Prezi and Keynote provide standards, guidance, and tips.

Activating the PDF
Interactive PDFs are a fresh, relatively new way to present reports and other softcopy documents, and they help create an engaging user experience.

PowerPointers

Ten tips for B2B branding in presentations:

1. Shape resonant brand experiences by relaying real-world examples, ideally through personal anecdotes.

2. Don't present books—try less show and more tell, which ascribes real value to the speaker.

3. Make use of colors and typography, but consider lighting and room size when setting standards that ensure optimal visibility.

4. Include agenda and break slides, which provide structure and can build anticipation.

5. Avoid filling the slides with text: achieve a 1:1:1 ratio between text, supporting graphics, and white space.

6. Use divider slides not just to break sections but to break the monotony.

7. Create a visual narrative, with aligned imagery that flows as fluidly as the text.

8. Don't overuse animation: the most important animation comes from the speaker. Motion, fades, and washes can be useful, but their overuse can be distracting and gimmicky.

9. Consider embedded hyperlinks to relevant websites or contacts, even for on-screen presentations; audience members often request copies for reference.

10. Close with purpose. Conclude your presentation with an audience call to action, summarized takeaways, or provocative thoughts or questions.

Presenting one look
As for PowerPoint, templates were created for Prezi and Keynote to guarantee a similar Deloitte experience no matter the software.

Brochureware

In the canon of B2B marketing-communications material, "brochureware" is one of the broadest and most high-profile categories. Increasingly recognized simply as vehicles for thought leadership, these branded applications are bound by more than binding. They are perspective deliverers and perspective shapers, helping to capture mindshare and, ultimately, "wallet-share."

While there are certainly some examples of B2C brochures, those in the B2B domain are far more common—and correspondingly more critical to shaping brand perceptions. After all, differentiators for most B2Bs are not conventional products. And when a physical good is being trafficked, it's often an undifferentiated commodity. For B2Bs, the product is an idea. An insight. A service. A solution.

Through carefully crafted words and design, brochures deliver distinct points of view as well as distinct experiences. They are commonly text-heavy, and rich in opportunities for influencing audience behavior.

The format runs counter to today's online communications—from e-mails to social media blasts—which customarily feature a minimum of designed components and short bursts of text. While these electronic communications may have reduced the quantity of brochures being developed, they have only increased the need for their denser content.

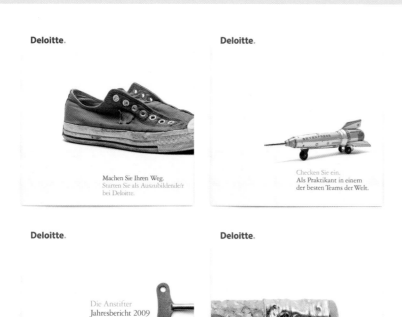

The breadth of the brochureware category underscores the importance of a consistent design approach. Whatever the subject matter, the ultimate Deloitte criterion —"focus"—helps to shape an optimal audience experience, with a clean presentation of content engendered by ample white space and a clear information hierarchy. There is, therefore, always an explicit link to the brand positioning, tone of voice, and messaging framework.

We faced the challenge of positioning one unified global strategic brand within a mosaic of cultures and markets in the Middle East. The brand value proposition in our brochureware told the story of a firm that can bring its global might to our clients' unique needs.

RANA SALHAB
Partner, Talent & Communications
Deloitte Middle East

Welcoming new employees
Deloitte Belgium and the 340 new branded cars

At the end of their first day in Deloitte, the main moment came: each of the newcomers received the keys of a Deloitte Branded Mini Cooper.

From colleague to Deloitte
The Deloitte International Student Business Forum

In your journey to the top, there are a few stops you should definitely make. The Deloitte International Student Business Forum is one of those destinations.

Myriad ideas, one identity
Deloitte brochureware has a consistent composition; logo, type, and imagery are all coordinated.

Magazines and newspapers

Extra! Extra! Read all about it! Periodicals, even in print form, continue to be highly effective means of delivering differentiated, leading-edge content. Failing to subscribe to this approach may not turn a B2B brand into yesterday's news, but it will help the competition get the headlines.

With the increasing commoditization of products and services, more and more of today's audiences are defining brands by the specific knowledge and insights they deliver. Magazines and newspapers provide an ideal forum for building on these associations through rapidly produced, issue-focused editorial content.

Their speed of delivery may not come close to that of social media's real-time connectivity, but neither do they come with its risks or content limitations. Regularly issued periodicals of consistent quality and character possess an inherent credibility. They can also create a hard to quantify—and hard to eclipse—sense of audience anticipation.

While the past few years have witnessed the rapid rise of e-newspapers and e-magazines, there has nonetheless been a minor renaissance in printed pieces. The movement of B2Bs back to traditional magazines and newspapers can be attributed to the glut of softcopy material, the challenges in reading content-heavy publications on smartphones, and, most interestingly, audience longing for a more traditional, tactile experience.

Finding information on any subject is no longer a problem. But are the available sources trustworthy? High-quality corporate magazines and newspapers that emphasize editorial content over promotional speech are increasingly recognized as the best sources of business knowledge. Back to basics!

HELOISA MONTES
Chief Strategy & Marketing Officer
Deloitte Brazil

The Pod

We get up close and personal with ...
Peter Devlin

Solventia

Nuevos caminos a explorar
Nuevas oportunidades ante
nuevos desafíos

DeloitteMatters

As One
Refreshing recipes
for growth

Link

Green Power.

dialog

Stammhirn
Schlau vernetzt

Up front

Leading the way in changing times
Insights for private equity

Mundo*Corporativo*

eza que vem de dentro
har sobre as regiões
entes do interior
sil

ítte.

 no de expansão

Mundo*Corporativo*

Sempre em movimento
Na corrida rumo a
um futuro ainda mais
competitivo

Deloitte.

Novos
tempos,
novos
papéis

Mundo*Corporativo*

Caminho sem volta
Passada a instabilidade,
é hora de se adaptar às
novas tendências

Deloitte.

Um salto para   o futuro

Point *of* View

ing/Failing to fail/plan

itte.

Middle East
Point *of* View

On the region's burning issues

Deloitte.

Middle East
Point *of* View

When it leaks...

Deloitte.

Facing up
to FATCA

What is the color
of your Strategy?

Back
to the
future

(Im)press: Brand-building magazine and newspaper design

- Design mastheads with care. They are the recurring component that binds the reader to the brand. Aligning color and typography with the identity system is critical.

- Avoid multiple page jumps. Asking readers to hunt around interrupts their concentration and jeopardizes the stories they must leapfrog.

- Make sure the reader can glean the gist of a story from a combination of headlines, subheads, and images. Subheads should be useful, not just afterthoughts used to break up the text. They should be visible, long, and informative.

- Extend images to the edge of the page to create a more striking layout. By ignoring the margins, a bleed disrupts the page design the reader expects.

- Exploit the contrast between vertically and horizontally oriented layouts. Playing them against each other creates interest, variety, and surprise.

- Vary pace and structure throughout a document through imagery, pull-quotes, and white space. Use asymmetry for compositional variety.

Bold and beautiful
Deloitte member firm business magazines, such as *Mundo Corporativo* in Brazil and *Point of View* in the Middle East, use vibrant color, vivid imagery, and unconventionally large font sizes to capture and keep audience attention.

Black and white and read all over
Inject energy and personality into newspapers through asymmetrical composition. While fluidity and balance are important, imagery and typography can be used creatively to engage the reader.

Reviews and reports

Annual reviews and reports, signature publications for B2B brands, are opportunities to communicate not just financial standings but the brand promise as well. Yesterday's predictable performance summaries are now augmented by richly composed, engaging, and comprehensive narratives that are highly effective for enhancing brand relevance and reputation.

Deloitte.

While these pieces are first and foremost platforms for delivering financial results to shareholders and other investors, they now reach a far wider audience, since reports are accessible to everyone via the internet. Communicating the brand personality necessitates using dynamic content, multimedia tools, and storytelling to add vibrancy and emotion.

As showpiece brand, marketing, communication, and even sales vehicles for B2Bs, reviews and reports require ample resources allotted to all components of their creation—from financials and text to visuals; from how these are compiled to how they are composed on the page. To help add richness and resonance to all of the elements, adopt a theme— the glue of the piece, binding the content and also connecting it to the business's brand. Make certain that the message being conveyed appears not only on the cover but is also interwoven throughout. It can be implicitly communicated, so long as the meaning is clear. . . and clearly tied back to the strategy and culture of the organization.

A Borderless Network
Deloitte 2011 Annual Review

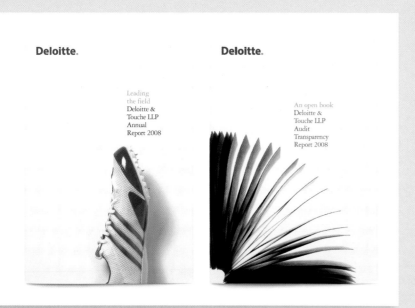

Many Deloitte member firms create their own annual reviews and reports, and some also generate function-specific pieces, such as those for Corporate Responsibility and Talent. But the Deloitte identity system always applies. Even though their scale and the resources allocated for delivering them can vary greatly, their look and feel remain distinctly Deloitte—focused, impactful messaging; authentic, personal stories; clearly conveyed data; and a minimalist, elegant design.

Branding and communication techniques now enliven what were once staid reports and reviews, which can therefore drive messages rather than merely provide information.

ATUL DHAWAN
Regional Managing Partner, Leader Clients & Markets
Deloitte India

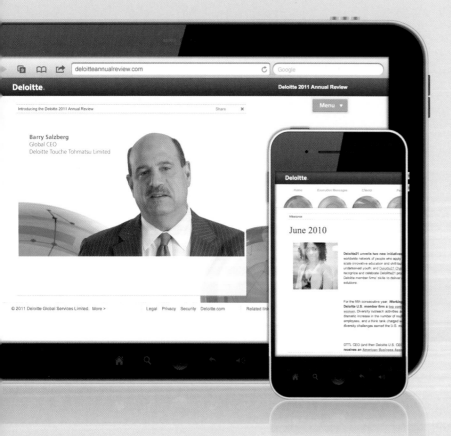

A new view of reviews
Mobile-friendly versions of reviews are encouraged. Embedded interactivity communicates results—and the brand—engagingly.

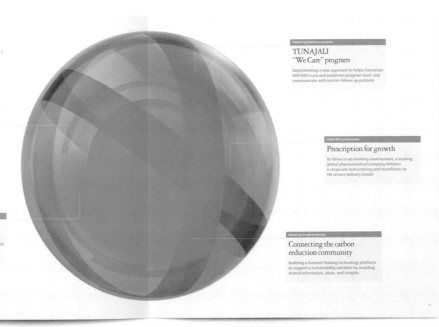

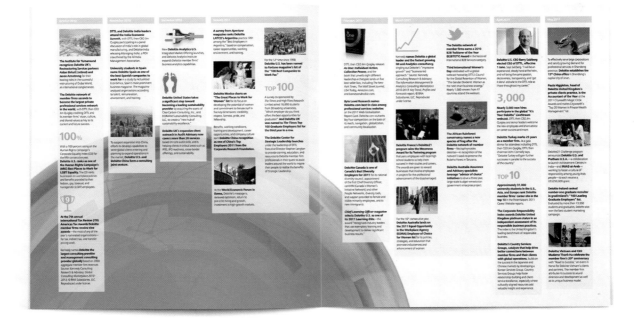

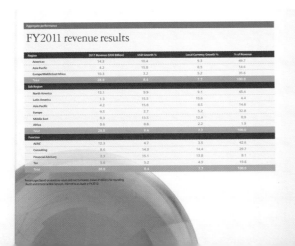

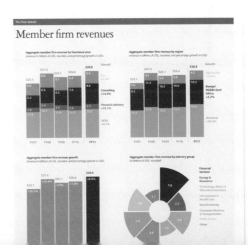

Proposals

The proposal document is the most concrete and comprehensive piece of branding produced during the proposal process. It will be seen by people at the client organization whom you never meet; it will be referred to throughout the decision-making process and recalled long after the selection is made. When there is little separating the competition, how the brand is expressed and experienced can make all the difference.

Few documents will impact B2B revenues as directly as those linked to a proposal. For the best chance of success, strategy, insight, and creativity need to inform not only the solution presented to the client but also the design of the proposal document itself. On its own, the piece will rarely win a job, but it can easily lose one, especially if it fails to demonstrate an understanding of the client and their situation.

Here, tailoring is everything. This is a challenge for B2Bs, which lean on generic template design and boilerplate content. Proposal documents must be as highly customized as resources allow.

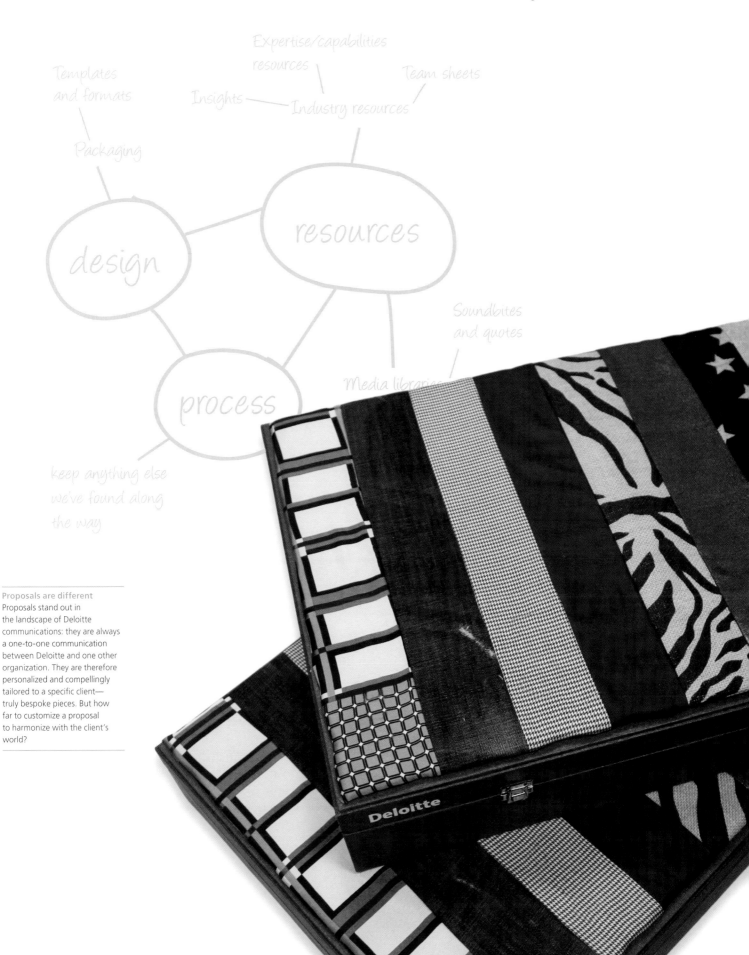

Templates
and formats

Packaging

Expertise/capabilities
resources

Insights ——— Industry resources

Team sheets

design

resources

process

Soundbites
and quotes

Media libraries

keep anything else
we've found along
the way

Proposals are different
Proposals stand out in
the landscape of Deloitte
communications: they are always
a one-to-one communication
between Deloitte and one other
organization. They are therefore
personalized and compellingly
tailored to a specific client—
truly bespoke pieces. But how
far to customize a proposal
to harmonize with the client's
world?

Proposals are brand ambassadors that can communicate quality and consistency at every turn. And brand ambassadors do more than just talk about brands; they foster rich, relevant, distinctive experiences. A theme is interwoven throughout all proposal components. It is visible in the words and images and inherent in the promise of the proposed solution. A comprehensive proposal toolkit, which includes a handbook, checklist, and style guide, articulates the organization-wide approach to communicating—and building—the Deloitte brand through all proposal-related interactions.

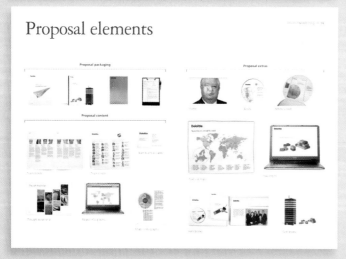

Each proposal is an ambassador for the Deloitte brand. Every aspect of its design should be planned and produced to achieve maximum effect and quality.

CARLOS MARTIN AMATE
Director, Communications, Image & Business Support
Deloitte Spain

Common proposal
characteristics
Three phases characterize all
proposals: prepare, execute,
and win. The three are equally
important—a lack of preparation
can create a chaotic impression;
poor execution is embarrassing
and hurts the Deloitte brand; and
failing to win, or at least leverage
the rapport built through the
proposal process, means member
firms can't capitalize on the time
and money spent pursuing the
opportunity.

Common proposal characteristics

Prepare	
1. Mobilize	Decide whether or not to pursue the opportunity and get the team off on the right foot
2. Understand	Get under the skin of the client and use the opportunity to better Deloitte's comparative competitive position
3. Plan	Develop a winning value proposition and make sure everyone on the proposal team understands who is doing what, and that the process maximizes client face time
Execute	
4. Interact	Take every opportunity to demonstrate our credentials, improve our understanding, and test The Deloitte Difference with the client
5. Articulate	Draft the document, circulate and incorporate changes, manage production to meet the client's schedule
6. Present	Agree on the presentation's focus, decide Deloitte participants and presentation medium, and plan for at least three rehearsal rounds
Win	
7. Follow up	Follow up while the decision is being made and continue client contact. Act immediately whether you have won or lost
8. Capitalize	Make the most of your investment by debriefing the team and the client, learning from what the client tells us, and developing an ongoing strategy to win work from the client

Make your proposals STAND OUT...

- **S**ource or commission unique, powerful imagery; avoid clichéd photos and graphics not inherently and insightfully linked to the topic.

- **T**heme your proposals thoughtfully; give them a distinctive, central idea that links all content, adds nuance, and makes the offer memorable.

- **A**ssociate conclusively the services offered with the brand offering them: leave no doubt that the proposal could only have come from your organization.

- **N**ever underestimate the power of the initial impression; clever, creative packaging can be an immediate differentiator and engender an expectation for the quality of service to come.

- **D**esign early; allowing designers to work closely with the business development and copywriting professionals will result in a more vivid articulation of the core offer.

- **O**btain permission to use elements of the client's brand, and apply them carefully; remember, no one is more protective of a client's brand than the client.

- **U**nderstand the presentation environment so materials can be shaped accordingly; variables such as room size, group size, and even lighting can influence the outcome.

- **T**ake advantage of interactive technology like the iPad and similar devices; they will enhance your proposal.

Packaging

Because it so often constitutes first-touch brand interaction, packaging has the power to influence not just behaviors, but perceptions. While the most important suggestion may be "please open me," wrappers—from containers to folders to simple paper—can go beyond shaping action and begin to shape opinion.

Though often an afterthought, the packaging of branded pieces is a critical component of the audience experience. It offers a brief opportunity to make a lasting impression, one that reflects the brand as much as the material it contains.

Packaging may be best defined by that which it envelops, which falls into two categories: business material and merchandise. But before considering the packaging's physical properties—paper or plastic, gloss or matte, heavy or lightweight, transparent or opaque—start with the intangibles. What is the feeling you want to trigger? What qualities do you want associated with the brand? Is it intelligence? Insightfulness? Innovation? Having answers to these questions long before the submission deadline will lead to the most auspicious brand experience. And effective packaging can convey a host of qualities. Once you decide on them, you can focus on the style in which to express them.

Guidelines for Deloitte-branded packaging are relatively sparse; professionals are encouraged to concentrate on two core elements: tone-of-voice and composition. Yet the consistency of the designs is amazing. Leaning on the organization's compositional creed—"focus"—yields modern, minimalist packaging, effectively communicates top-line ideas, and advances impressions of authority, elegance, creativity, and a host of other intangibles. Deloitte's compositional standards manifest this personality, achieving a pleasing balance through ample use of white space, asymmetry, and a simple, informational hierarchy.

While the Deloitte logo must appear on all the organization's material, packaging provides a rare opportunity to emphasize supporting visual attributes and deemphasize the logo. Color and typography get the most play. For the former, understated white, blue, and green wrappers not only correctly position the item, they are also cost-effective. And for the latter, simple yet provocative messaging is delivered through Deloitte's signature typography, either as isolated phrases or as elements in a tiled or wallpaper vista.

Truly distinctive packaging can influence decisions, especially when it produces a sensorial and emotional connection with the client.

LORENA TORRES
Director, Marketing
Deloitte Mexico

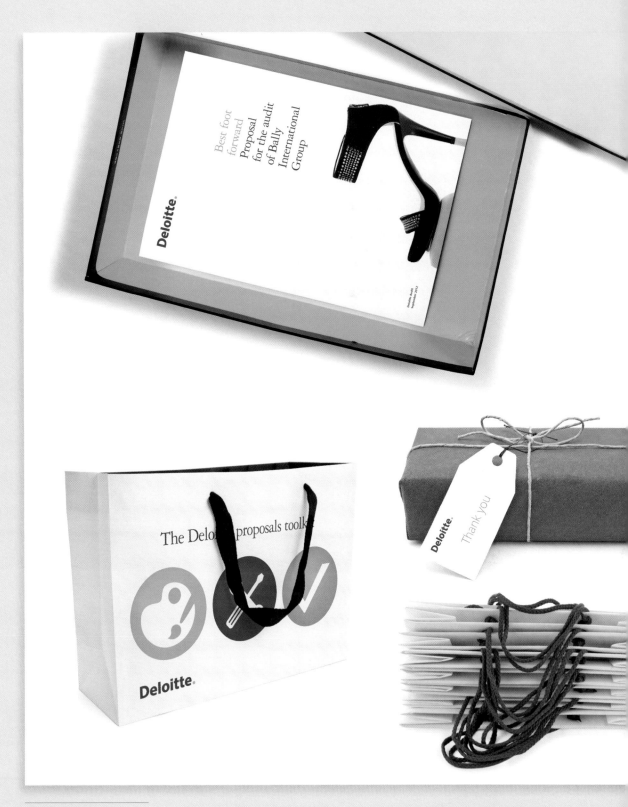

The complete package
With every wrapper, folder, container, or case, consider the entire audience experience—the physical as well as the emotional.

One-time materials

Posters, flyers, leaflets, invitations, and display cards form a menagerie of corporate marketing material related by unconventional sizing and a rapid production cycle. What is most unconventional and rapid about such pieces, however, is their ability—when given appropriate emphasis—to reinforce the brand promise.

There is no denying the profile, reach, and impact of annual reports, brochures, and advertisements. But through sheer quantity, one-time printed materials can shape the brand experience significantly. Consistency is therefore critical. Whether used to promote an event, drive traffic to a website, or simply make an internal announcement, such pieces must leverage the core elements of the visual identity and also reflect the organization's personality. Their variable sizes and composition mean they are difficult to template; this makes paramount marcom's and design's understanding of the need for brand alignment.

Deloitte considers one-time printed materials the front door not only for events, programs, and initiatives but also for a brand experience. A piece created in isolation is a lost opportunity. This is why all Deloitte invitations, posters, and flyers strive to reinforce the value of the entire brand. This is customarily accomplished through the prominent placement of the Deloitte logo; by applying the standard color palette and fonts; and by using striking, symbolic imagery. Personalizing the material for the recipients, when appropriate, further strengthens the brand voice and improves marketplace visibility.

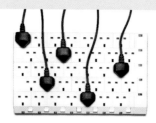

Deloitte.

Get connected
Global partners
meeting 2008
San Jose, USA

Deloitte.

Untangling the web
Breakfast seminar

Tuesday 25 November 2008, 8.30am
Catherine Guirguis will discuss how to
simplify IT compliance for clients.

Inviting attention
Consider the following when creating invitations for roundtables, workshops, recruiting fairs, and other B2B events:

- Match the design of the invite (e.g., elegant and text-heavy, engaging and illustrated, etc.) with the nature of the event (e.g., formal and structured, informal and fun, etc.).

- Mirror the theme of the event itself in the invitation.

- Use a URL or QR-like code to connect invitees to supporting materials; invitations are not books.

- Think about the tactile components of the piece, including paper stock (light or heavy), finish (gloss or matte) and type (foil, embossing, etc.).

- Design the envelope as a complement to the invitation.

- Do not sacrifice function for form: prominently feature key information such as date, venue, and RSVP.

Identification cards
Tent and display cards, posters, and leaflets prominently display the Deloitte brand identity while simultaneously conveying key, topic-specific information.

Thank you for
your patience
during this
long period of
refurbishment.

Deloitte.

Pop up and see us
New cafe now open
on the 2nd floor

Deloitte.

A real page turner
Deloitte Book Club

Deloitte.

Join the party
New partners
dinner 2008

Thursday 2 December 2008
London, United Kingdom

Deloitte.

An evening
of refinement
Oil industry
reception

Deloitte.

Looking ahead to 2009?
Get an in-depth view

Launch of TMT Predictions 2009
A personal invitation

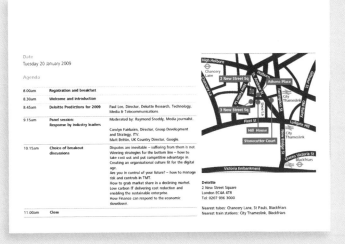

Date
Tuesday 20 January 2009

Agenda

Time		Detail
8.00am	Registration and breakfast	
8.30am	Welcome and introduction	
8.45am	Deloitte Predictions for 2009	Paul Lee, Director, Deloitte Research, Technology, Media & Telecommunications
9.15am	Panel session: Response by industry leaders	Moderated by: Raymond Snoddy, Media journalist. Carolyn Fairbairn, Director, Group Development and Strategy, ITV. Matt Brittin, UK Country Director, Google.
10.15am	Choice of breakout discussions	Disputes are inevitable – suffering from them is not. Winning strategies for the bottom line – how to take cost out and put competitive advantage in. Creating an organisational culture fit for the digital age. Are you in control of your future? – how to manage risk and controls in TMT. How to grab market share in a declining market. Low carbon IT delivering cost reduction and enabling the sustainable enterprise. How Finance can respond to the economic slowdown.
11.00am	Close	

Deloitte
2 New Street Square
London EC4A 4TR
Tel: 0207 936 3000

Nearest tubes: Chancery Lane, St Pauls, Blackfriars
Nearest train stations: City Thameslink, Blackfriars

Inviting attention
One-time materials such as these
invitations strike a balance between
representing the Deloitte brand,
illustrating the event's theme, and
meeting audience needs.

Advertising

"Oh, you mean advertising?" is a common response to the mention of branding to those not well-versed in the field. Branding is, of course, much more than advertising. But advertising is not much more than branding—it is a way to deliver a consistent experience in a targeted and compelling way to external marketplaces.

Advertisements are not just for consumer products; they are among the most high-profile and high-cost expressions of B2B brands. Their visibility and accessibility invite attention from key stakeholders, both inside and outside the organization. They must therefore represent the best of brand positioning and personality.

Some ads are created primarily to inform, introduce, or reinforce; others are designed to provoke. Whatever their function, advertisements always influence perception of the brand. Whether you are creating a one-time, one-channel communication or developing a holistic campaign across many channels, to maximize the value of your ads, consider the broader brand experience—ask, in other words, not just "What does this say about my organization?" but also "What will people now say about my organization?"

A black whole (Australia)
The Deloitte global Green Dot Campaign launched in Australia in 2009. Since that first newspaper placement, Green Dot ads—noted for their bold, black canvas and thought-provoking application of the dot—have appeared in over 100 countries. They can be found to this day, vivid in newspapers and on websites and exterior signage.

In late 2009, Deloitte unveiled the Green Dot Campaign, a global communications initiative that, in a powerful, dedicated way, expressed the organization's point of view on the issues and opportunities facing our clients and our recruits. As always, shaping these advertisements were the principle of "focus" and the "Always One Step Ahead" legacy brand positioning.

The design was simple yet bold, with Deloitte's iconic Green Dot as the hero set against a black background. The combination captured the clarity, leadership, and direction of the Deloitte point of view in a unique and unforgettable way, and cut through the clutter on websites and in publications.

For the Deloitte member firms to contribute to a unified, effective campaign, the construct had to be adaptable to their own cultures and locations. Its malleability led to the most successful campaign in the history of the network, with over 200 different ads run in over 100 countries.

YouTube and the YouTube logo are registered trademarks of Google Inc., used with permission.

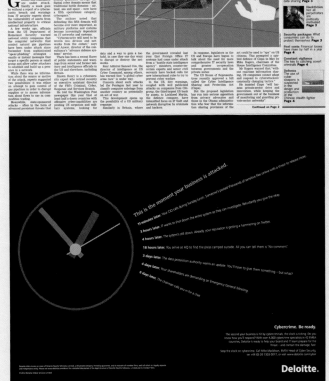

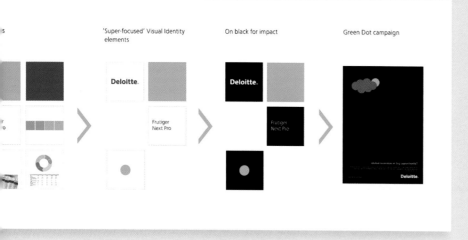

Our Green Dot campaign works so well because it's so simple that our people feel they could have done it themselves; they therefore feel connected to it, proud of it, and want to contribute to it. It's an easy campaign to love. On another level it's timeless, like great, minimalist art: classic, understated, iconic, and stripped down to the fundamental elements of color, symbol, and message—synonyms for cut-through, memorable advertising.

DAVID REDHILL
Partner and Chief Marketing Officer
Deloitte Australia

The A-to-Zs of ads
Agencies and internal professionals receive comprehensive guidance on creating campaign ads. It emphasizes the appropriate use of all design elements as well as more subjective components, such as the meaning of the Green Dot and what constitutes effective tone of voice.

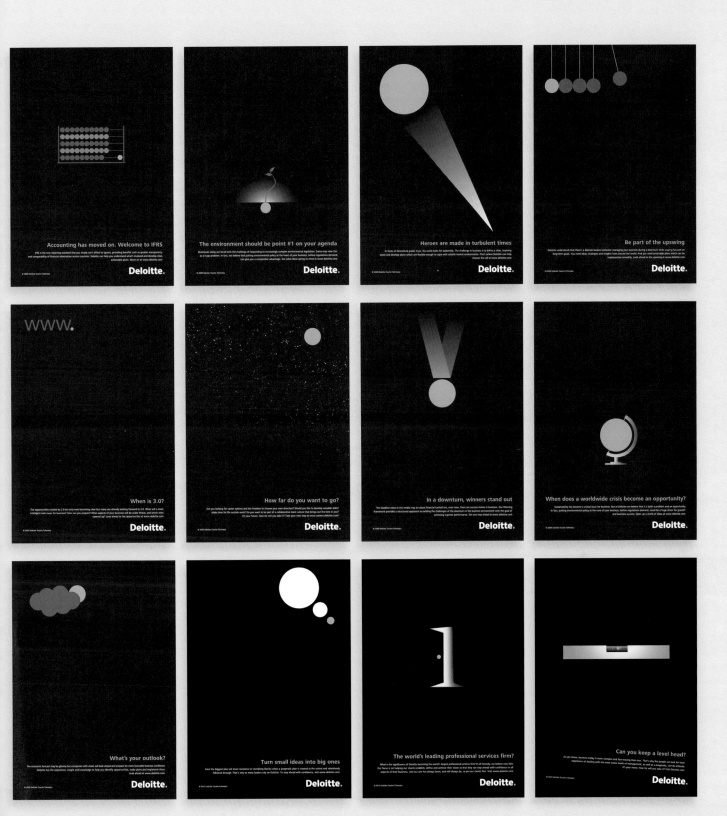

Tools for success
The Green Dot Campaign was launched along with a toolbox that facilitates its consistent application worldwide. This included an initial suite of advertisements and comprehensive guidance for new treatments locally.

Sponsorships

Sponsorships can be powerful tools for strengthening—or shifting—perceptions and reputation. In an era of shared media and shared opinion, these marketing and promotional associations enable B2Bs to connect with a wider audience; when cleverly constructed, they not only start conversations, they change them.

As channels and methods of communication have evolved, so too has the nature of sponsorships. Digital forums for interaction—most prominently, social media—have elevated their profile and potential (as well as making the measurement of their impact more accurate). Whether the brand is associated with an individual or an entity, the speed, authenticity, and transparency of today's communications are making it easier to enhance marketplace positioning.

But social media also make it easier to damage reputation. Sponsorships can be risky, as businesses can quickly become guilty by association when problems arise for partners. Ample due diligence and risk-mitigation planning are always in order before entering into a sponsorship. In many ways, their brand becomes your own, so the association should be treated with as much care as you would treat your own brand.

As brand purpose becomes more influential, many top B2B organizations are emphasizing community programs over celebrity sponsorships. And as such programs receive more and more attention, B2Bs are changing their approach to them. The cash donations of old are being replaced by the provision of resources and business expertise, with core products and services themselves used to demonstrate the power to positively impact society.

Horse play
In Argentina, Deloitte leverages the hugely popular national sport of polo for a positive brand association. The sponsorship is brought to life through a wide array of site-specific signage and merchandise.

Sponsorship decisions made by member firms help align them with local markets and resources. Alongside these relationships there are a select number of worldwide strategic alliances, such as those with the World Economic Forum and the United Nations Global Compact; these emphasize business's positive contributions to society. On the local level, there are many affiliations with community programs. And for certain signature events in sports, entertainment, and the arts, member firms engage in alliances that position them as "the official provider" or "professional services provider of choice."

Deloitte's brand identity remains consistent, regardless of the sponsorship. The logo is the visual showpiece of the affiliation, always present in unadulterated fashion, never locked to third-party marks or identifiers. Wherever possible, the other core components of the identity system—color, type, and imagery—are applied as they would be internally. And beyond onsite signage, advertising, partnered thought leadership, and other co-branded materials, the sponsorship agreements may also enable third-party branded assets to be grafted onto Deloitte material; there are clear compositional guidelines for such instances as well.

B2B sponsorship is about much more than logo placement. It's a showcase for your brand—what you can deliver, what you believe in, what you stand for as an organization.

ANNABEL PRITCHARD
Director, Brand & Marketing
Deloitte United Kingdom

From the field of play to the field of plays
The Deloitte brand can be seen and experienced through all sorts of sponsorships, extending beyond the traditional sports teams.

Teaming to win

A constant of Deloitte-branded sponsorships is a commitment to quality and mutuality. An "as one" approach, brought to life through team sports and group activities, is a hallmark.

Electronic communications

In a few years—perhaps months, or maybe even today—"electronic communications" will cease to exist. This is not meant to suggest a shift away from digital tools and vehicles, but rather that *all* primary communications will be electronic. Much like "e-commerce" is now an antiquated term—we now refer to it simply as "commerce,"—"electronic communications" is fast becoming "communication."

Electronic communications encompasses everything from web and mobile sites to wallpaper, screensavers, and a wide array of branded e-templates. The platforms themselves, including social media, will be covered in upcoming chapters; here, the focus is on tools. In this arena, consider both form and function. For the B2B brand clear on—and committed to—the online experiences it is trying to conjure, it is critical to emphasize both.

Here, form indicates the look and feel of a brand's communications. Are they consistently rendered? Do they highlight the brand identity's best properties? Will they capture audience attention? Function covers end-user experience. Does the communication leverage the interactive features offered by all operating systems? Is navigation easy and intuitive? Does it reward the audience for their time?

e-asy for e-veryone
Deloitte-branded
e-communication templates are
accessible to all professionals.
HTML and noncoded, system-
based equivalents ensure
consistent application.

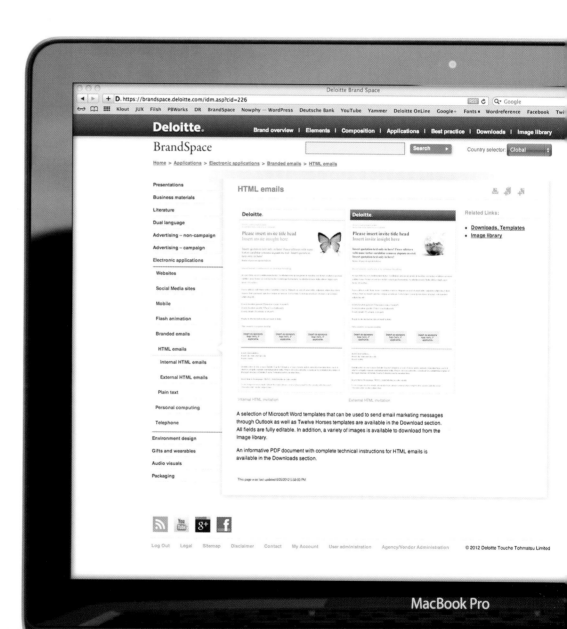

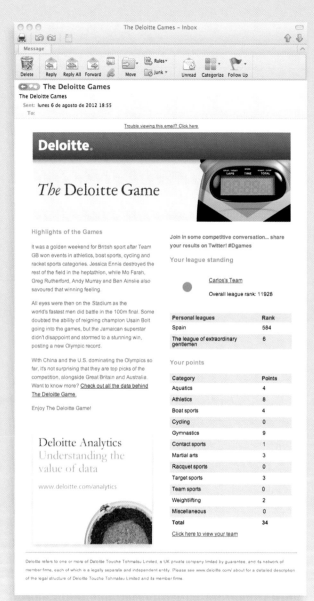

The positioning of all Deloitte-branded electronic communications was shaped by the positioning of the Deloitte brand itself. Being "Always One Step Ahead"—and providing that experience for clients and talent—served as an effective mantra for shaping it centrally and activating it locally.

In brand asset management, the concept of "anticipation" speaks to the development of tools and guidance for today's technology as well as tomorrow's; "pragmatism" governs the construction of templates and functional material that would result in an intuitive end-user experience; and "relentlessness" relates to the influence of local professionals, not just in applying the brand electronically with consistency, but also in providing useful feedback and recommendations that continue to fuel the evolution of the Deloitte identity.

We are seeing a radical shift from offline to online communications. Online channels, including social media, are now our primary means of sharing content with all target audiences.

MIREILLE SPAPENS
Director Brand, Communications & Corporate Responsibility
Deloitte Netherlands

Ingredients for integration
A digital communications strategy is more than fusing an "e-" to everything. A holistic approach leads to the clear, seamless integration of all components.

Channels	Vehicles	Enablers	Reinforcers
Website	General e-mail	Icons	Screen saver
Mobile	Newsletters	QR codes	Wallpaper
Social	Invitations	Multimedia	Phone/Voice mail

Name Surname
Title | Name of service line/Industry/Department
Deloitte legal entity
Address, Street, City, State, Post code, Country
Tel/Direct: +00 (0)00 0000 0000 | Fax: +00 (0)00 0000 0000 | Mo
name@deloitte.com | www.deloitte.com

Please consider the environment before printing.

The YouTube, Facebook, Twitter, and Google+ logos are trademarks of their respective owners, and their inclusion in the screen shots shown here is not intended to suggest any authorization or endorsement.

Websites

Until recently, measuring the success of a B2B website was usually as crude as counting page visits. But more sophisticated interpretations of what online success means have come with more sophisticated measures. More important than the number of times people visit is who they are, where they came from, and what they do once they enter the business's virtual world.

Page hits, as historically defined, no longer possess huge value. The number of file requests from a website is good to know, but it is a flawed and limited metric. More up-to-date measures tell a different tale—one of successful interactions with online content that generate positive and distinct experiences and lead to further connections.

These are page hits that matter. They do not replace the traditional metrics of site traffic, lead generation, and increased sales and network community, but they do enhance those measures by digging deeper to identify behavioral drivers. Once these triggers are clearly discerned, the progressive B2B organization can shape user journeys with experiences equal parts rich, robust, and rewarding.

Effective website design—or, more specifically, brand design via website design—depends on a solid understanding of the audience. Who is being targeted? Ultimate decision-makers or those who influence them? Students or experienced hires? Shareholders or analysts? Armed with answers, you will make much better choices as to how to handle the brand positioning, based on knowledge of the audience's preferences for taking in the website's content.

For instance, it is becoming increasingly common for audiences to turn to B2B sites only after they have visited independent aggregator or delivery sites. This makes brand presence on third-party channels all the more important. It's less hub-and-spoke, more entanglement; less pull, more push.

Dot uncommon
The Deloitte.com website has won multiple awards for its clean, intuitive interface; rich multimedia content; and strong cross-channel, cross-border integration.

Deloitte-branded websites—winners of multiple awards in the B2B category—share basic layout and navigation conventions and an overall look and feel. This consistency extends beyond "on-platform" sites to career and social media channels. While most Deloitte-branded sites feature some distinct design and functional features, the objective is to create a consistent, trusted, rewarding online experience across all sites, whether they're internal or external. The content and layout for all new webpage designs—especially those "off-platform"—must always be relevant, potent, and in keeping with the basic brand guidelines.

Guiding the style guide

To ensure consistency of design, brand representation, and end-user experience, consider furnishing guidance, downloadable files, and style sheets for the following elements:

- **Personality:** How is the brand identity articulated so it conveys the essence of the organization?

- **Composition:** How do the design elements interact for maximum impact?

- **Logo:** Where does it appear? How is it sized? Is it clickable? Is it a favicon?

- **Color:** What tints are acceptable? Where are they to be applied? What gradations and beveling are acceptable?

- **Fonts:** Is there a type hierarchy? How are headlines treated? What about body copy? Captions? Hyperlinks?

- **Imagery:** What are the standard styles and sizing for lead images? Headshots? Thumbnails?

- **Multimedia:** Is the site Flash-enabled? Does it employ closed captioning? How fast are the transition speeds? What audio cues are used?

- **Actions:** How are standard navigational buttons, drop-down menus, hyperlinks, and rollovers integrated?

Today, the end users are in the driver's seat. It's up to B2B brands to provide them with what they want, when they want it, how they want it. If your organization can't meet that challenge, someone else's certainly will.

BILL BARRETT
Director, Online Communications
Deloitte Touche Tohmatsu Limited

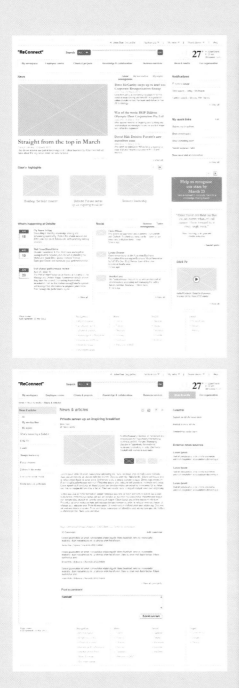

A need to "now" basis
Deloitte member firms keep all their
professionals apprised of news and
information through a sophisticated
intranet, like this example from the
Australian member firm.

Mobile apps

Mobile apps are the flavor of the month, even in the B2B space. They offer a potent mix of portability, accessibility, and interactivity, enabling companies to connect with audiences in new, truly powerful ways. Their promise has business leaders scrambling to fast-forward the development of a wide array of apps—when they should, in fact, be hitting the pause button.

If the old proverb "Nothing is certain but death and taxes" were given a makeover by a contemporary B2B marketing professional, it would probably read "Nothing is certain but that my bosses will be telling me they need an app." A mobile strategy is essential for B2Bs—mobile apps, less so. The executives trying to distinguish their brand should first distinguish between mobile strategy and apps. Reliably, they want the former but ask for the latter, thinking they are synonymous. This is not totally surprising. Nor is it as disheartening as it may at first seem.

The good news is that there is an understanding of the opportunity at hand. Or rather, *in* hand. Target audiences are using smartphones for tasks such as calling, texting, e-mailing, and conducting online transactions; tablets, used for surfing the web and accessing interactive media, are becoming a necessity for business executives and students alike. They are incredibly personal devices, leading to incredibly personal interactions with content and the brands that provide it.

Reimagining app functionality
The Deloitte Reimagining Business mobile app facilitates dialogue between member firm professionals and their clients about their business and its positive contributions to society.

Just as a cornerstone of brand strategy should be a clear comprehension of how audiences want and/or need to interact with your organization, mobile strategy requires an in-depth understanding of user preferences. Before focusing on devices and design, determine what content will deliver the most value. The most memorable and rewarding experiences often revolve around time-sensitive information, geo-based content, or a personalized VIP offer. Perhaps information about upcoming events, podcasts, or trade and industry shows will be of interest; maybe it's a webinar or real-time launch of a new product or service offering. When well executed, such interactions provide users with faster access to specific content in an interactive and engaging medium. They also build relationships, establish trust, and enhance reputation.

Mobile phones are deeply personal devices. People's attachment to them transcends the benefits of being able to make calls or surf the web on the go. It is therefore incredibly important to get the user experience right.

FRANK FARRALL
Lead Partner
Deloitte Digital Australia

Deloitte MeetingTime
This Deloitte-branded mobile app is designed to help business professionals recapture one of their most valuable commodities: time. A simple trick of the eye and mind helps audiences use MeetingTime more efficiently, allowing them to reallocate saved minutes or even hours to other pursuits.

Vendor selection

Do you want to conduct your mobile initiative in-house or with outside assistance? Do you want to hire an agency, a software vendor, or both? Most B2Bs lack the DIY capabilities. The questions below will guide the vendor selection process.

- How do setup costs compare to the specific channels under consideration?

- What are the ongoing management costs or other service fees?

- Is monitoring and measuring the technology included in the services?

- What is the vendor's stance on user privacy?

- What user data will be collected through the mobile app?

- What safeguards will protect intellectual property?

- Will this vendor respond to bug fixes for apps?

- Can the vendor provide ongoing maintenance for mobile sites?

- What level of quality assurance and testing will the vendor provide?

- How will the project be launched?

- How will the project be wrapped up?

- Is ongoing technical support available?

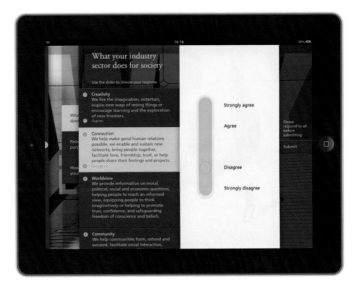

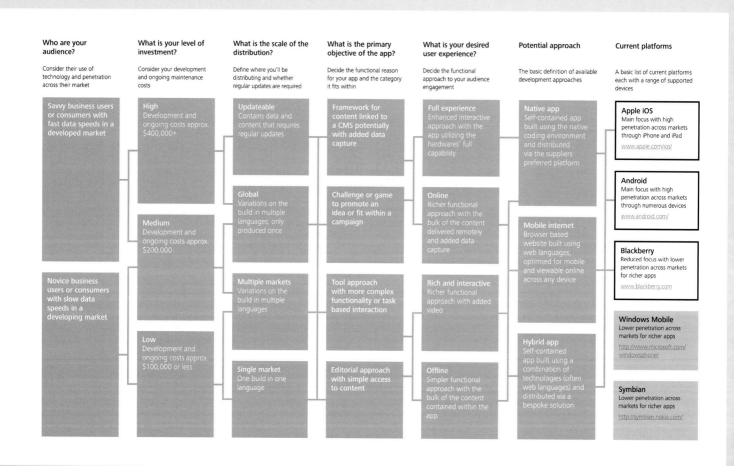

Who are your audience?	What is your level of investment?	What is the scale of the distribution?	What is the primary objective of the app?	What is your desired user experience?	Potential approach	Current platforms
Consider their use of technology and penetration across their market	Consider your development and ongoing maintenance costs	Define where you'll be distributing and whether regular updates are required	Decide the functional reason for your app and the category it fits within	Decide the functional approach to your audience engagement	The basic definition of available development approaches	A basic list of current platforms each with a range of supported devices

Who are your audience?
Consider their use of technology and penetration across their market

Savvy business users or consumers with fast data speeds in a developed market

Novice business users or consumers with slow data speeds in a developing market

What is your level of investment?
Consider your development and ongoing maintenance costs

High
Development and ongoing costs approx. $400,000+

Medium
Development and ongoing costs approx. $200,000

Low
Development and ongoing costs approx. $100,000 or less

What is the scale of the distribution?
Define where you'll be distributing and whether regular updates are required

Updateable
Contains data and content that requires regular updates

Global
Variations on the build in multiple languages; only produced once

Multiple markets
Variations on the build in multiple languages

Single market
One build in one language

What is the primary objective of the app?
Decide the functional reason for your app and the category it fits within

Framework for content linked to a CMS potentially with added data capture

Challenge or game to promote an idea or fit within a campaign

Tool approach with more complex functionality or task based interaction

Editorial approach with simple access to content

What is your desired user experience?
Decide the functional approach to your audience engagement

Full experience
Enhanced interactive approach with the app utilizing the hardwares' full capability

Online
Richer functional approach with the bulk of the content delivered remotely and added data capture

Rich and interactive
Richer functional approach with added video

Offline
Simpler functional approach with the bulk of the content contained within the app

Potential approach
The basic definition of available development approaches

Native app
Self-contained app built using the native coding environment and distributed via the suppliers preferred platform

Mobile internet
Browser based website built using web languages, optimised for mobile and viewable online across any device

Hybrid app
Self-contained app built using a combination of technologies (often web languages) and distributed via a bespoke solution

Current platforms
A basic list of current platforms each with a range of supported devices

Apple iOS
Main focus with high penetration across markets through iPhone and iPad
www.apple.com/ios/

Android
Main focus with high penetration across markets through numerous devices
www.android.com/

Blackberry
Reduced focus with lower penetration across markets for richer apps
www.blackberry.com

Windows Mobile
Lower penetration across markets for richer apps
http://www.microsoft.com/windowsphone/

Symbian
Lower penetration across markets for richer apps
http://symbian.nokia.com/

Defining the best approach
With a range of different technical approaches, platforms, and devices, it's a challenge to choose the most appropriate for your requirements.

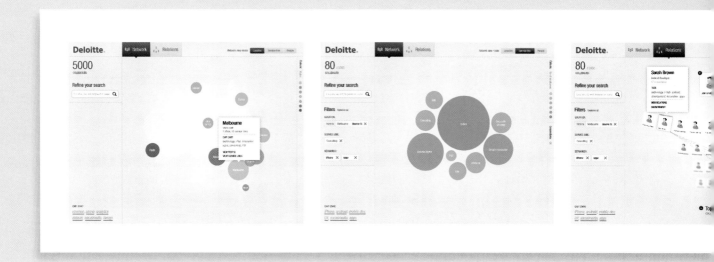

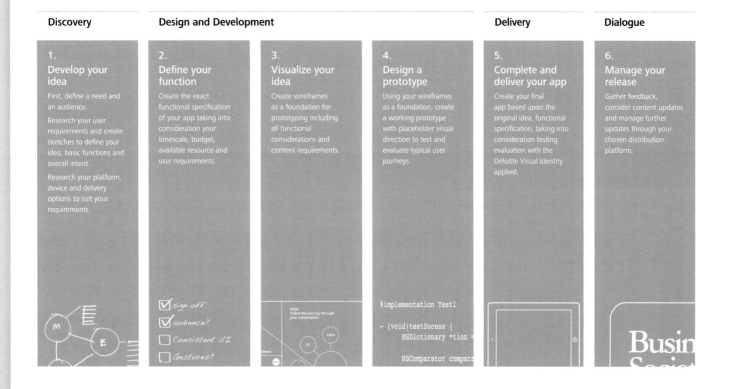

Discovery

Design and Development

Delivery

Dialogue

1.
Develop your idea

First, define a need and an audience.

Research your user requirements and create sketches to define your idea, basic functions and overall intent.

Research your platform, device and delivery options to suit your requirements.

2.
Define your function

Create the exact functional specification of your app taking into consideration your timescale, budget, available resource and user requirements.

3.
Visualize your idea

Create wireframes as a foundation for prototyping including all functional considerations and content requirements.

4.
Design a prototype

Using your wireframes as a foundation, create a working prototype with placeholder visual direction to test and evaluate typical user journeys.

5.
Complete and deliver your app

Create your final app based upon the original idea, functional specification, taking into consideration testing evaluation with the Deloitte Visual Identity applied.

6.
Manage your release

Gather feedback, consider content updates and manage further updates through your chosen distribution platform.

Understanding the process
From discovery to delivery, designing an app means following certain steps. Work within a defined structure and meet each step's requirements for the best possible outcome.

Social Media

Social-media channels are evolving. Fast. Faster than businesses can handle. Faster than guidelines and standards can be updated. They're nuanced, complex, and come with significant risk. In so many ways, social media is decidedly un-corporate and antiestablishment. Which is exactly why it's where today's established corporations need to be.

Relationship building. Connectivity. Authenticity. Trust. These ideas are at the heart of social media, just as they are at the heart of B2B brand-building. Until recently, only the most forward-thinking business leaders realized this. However, the symbiosis between social media and brand is now widely understood, and the former is regularly being leveraged to benefit the latter. B2Bs and their employees are using social-media channels to cultivate deeper relationships both inside and outside the organization; to build community, thereby networking like-minded individuals for problem-solving and sharing ideas; and to message, via traditional promotional and marketing campaigns or more intimate, real-time dialogue.

In all cases, the emphasis is on the individual. It's not that business is being *de*-emphasized; only that when B2B brands express themselves through social channels, they do so in a very human way—with personality, with honesty, and with immediacy. This approach is also hastening the demise of the antiquated perspective that social media is just a talent show.

Social media continues to be a great tool for recruiting, career-building, and networking. But businesses are increasingly tapping these channels for sales, marketing, and public relations, as well as to publicize their community-oriented good works. Independent of the channel, audience, and tactic, the brand focus should be on the ultimate delivery of value, communicated in a manner true to the organization's positioning and personality.

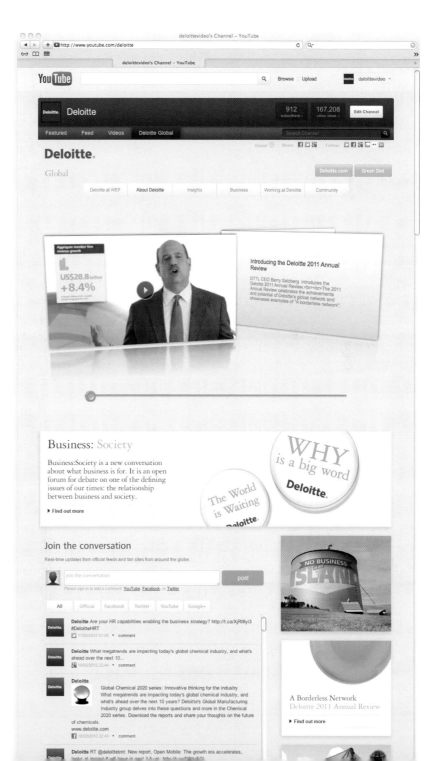

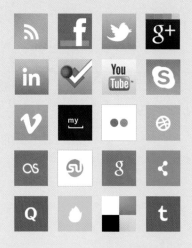

Social media has resulted in a fundamental change in the way Deloitte professionals interact with clients, talent, and each other. The spirit of social media—authentic, nonhierarchical, open, interactive—aligns perfectly with the brand and business of Deloitte; this is why most member firms permit the use of these channels. Governance does, of course, exist in order to protect Deloitte member firms' clients, people, and brands. Offices in various countries have published internal white papers, standards documents, and educational video series. But the primary piece of guidance communicated by all countries? Use common sense.

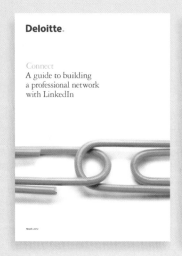

So far, social
Deloitte member firms and their professionals represent the brand with both quality and consistency across social-media channels. A range of guidebooks exist to help educate on the individual platforms.

The YouTube, Facebook, Twitter, and Google+ logos are trademarks of their respective owners, and their inclusion in the screen shots shown here is not intended to suggest any authorization or endorsement

Companies that develop social-media or social-business strategies need to align them with their business strategies; if they are isolated activities, they will fail before they launch.

ANDRE HUGO
Director
Deloitte Digital Africa

The YouTube, Facebook, Twitter, and Google+ logos are trademarks of their respective owners, and their inclusion in the screen shots shown here is not intended to suggest any authorization or endorsement

Audiovisuals

Action! The traditional direction to begin filming has never been more relevant. Today's audiences—more time-starved and ADD-afflicted than ever—are demanding that business content be delivered in new and dynamic ways. Which places audiovisual and multimedia vehicles in the spotlight. They are helping B2B brands connect with their stakeholders fast, with charisma and authenticity.

The dimensions of sound and motion make it challenging to establish guidelines for audiovisual pieces. The problem is often compounded by a rapid production cycle and the contributions of specialized outside vendors not fluent in the business's brand system. Organization-wide guidance for the creation of audiovisual material must therefore be clear, concise, and grounded in the brand identity's core assets. A less prescriptive approach may be counterintuitive for a medium with an abundance of moving parts, but the assortment of creative treatments, footage styles, and related technology soon evinces why "less is more" is the way to go.

In a time-poor business world where audiovisual communication is rapidly increasing, the challenge is to create brand-consistent material that gets to the heart of the message as quickly and simply as possible.

TONI HAMILTON
Director, Film & Multimedia
Deloitte Australia

All Deloitte-branded audiovisual content is guided primarily by the cornerstones of the entire visual system: the idea of "focus" and the familiar visual elements. Because of the wide array of postproduction styles that are an essential part of multimedia treatments, there is an especial emphasis on the consistent use of branded components such as bumpers (introductory/closing animated logo), titles, captions, and information graphics. This gives Deloitte member firm professionals the freedom to use a wider variety of footage styles while still maintaining a strong and clearly branded look and feel.

    Enjoy the break!

Better reception
B2B audiovisual vehicles are going beyond the "talking head" corporate videos of old. Better technology and in-house capabilities are combining with a better understanding of the audience to deliver high-quality, high-impact videos and multimedia brand experiences.

Content styles

There are four primary styles of footage in the Deloitte canon:

White style or object-based footage
Utilizes cutout imagery; consists of sharp focus, color footage or stills with symbolic or metaphoric relevance

Motion graphics footage
Professionally created 2-D and 3-D animation; fully utilizes color and iconographical brand elements, and is particularly useful for representing complex or abstract themes

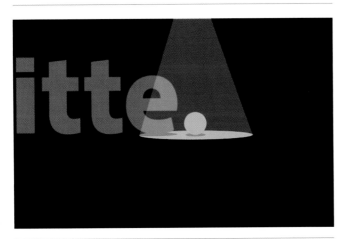

2-D animation footage
Uses flat graphics and simple movements to create clear, direct messages; usually created in-house and suited for rapid, online consumption

Students at the office
Deloitte Japan

Real-life footage
Full-color, reportage style; used to show people, events, places, and in some circumstances, industries

Film real
Different styles of footage and composition are bound to the Deloitte brand through an authentic, focused approach and by adhering to a small suite of recognizable identity assets.

Office environments

An increasingly mobile B2B workforce does not mean that less thought and resources should go into office environments. In fact, they've never been more critical to professional life. The workplace serves as an anchor, tethering employees and clients to the organization and concretizing the brand experience.

Office environments are all about signs. Not logos, banners, and navigational aids, but the work space itself. It provides essential indicators to employees, clients, recruits, and other visitors that they are connected to something. That "something" is the brand.

An effectively branded environment has been proven to influence behavior, build camaraderie, and contribute to staff productivity and happiness. It can convey intelligence and innovation to prospective clients, and demonstrate warmth and distinction to prospective talent.

A nice reception
The welcome and waiting
environments of Deloitte member
firm offices are designed to
convey a clear and comforting
sense of place.

The unified look and feel of the work environment contributes to productivity and pride of place, and in turn contributes to and reinforces pride in the brand.

TRACEY EDWARDS
Managing Director, Global Business Services & Chief Knowledge Officer
Deloitte Touche Tohmatsu Limited

Deloitte offices in Neuilly, France
The brand's signature green color is used to reinforces the organization's visual identity and adds energy and character to the office environment.

Deloitte offices in Viña del Mar, Chile
The clean, minimalist design is enhanced through the use of both natural and artificial lighting, which are both functional and aesthetically pleasing.

Deloitte member firms take great care in crafting workplaces that foster collaboration and innovation while simultaneously reinforcing the brand personality. The identity system is extended organically, with the color palette, typography, and imagery styles applied in intelligent, functional ways. In addition, high-quality, natural materials are used; lighting is area-appropriate and optimized for productivity and mood; maximum decibel levels are set for ambient noise and multimedia displays; and interactive terminals like touch screens are provided, along with traditional features like pin walls for sharing personal posts.

Deloitte offices in London and Prague
Though in different countries, these spaces are unmistakably related; they combine the Deloitte color palette with a bold application of glass and angular display.

TOP LEFT
Touch-screen news wall, New York

BOTTOM LEFT
Brand display cube, Rotterdam

BOTTOM RIGHT
Vending machines, Madrid

Signs of the times
Office signage is an opportunity for shaping brand experience, overtly via navigation, as well as through an implicit connection to the corporate identity.

If you think talent
can't be measured,
ask our clients
about their results

Deloitte.

The age-old
conical metal
device grooved in
an advancing
spiral, with a
head,
in other words,
a screw

Deloitte.

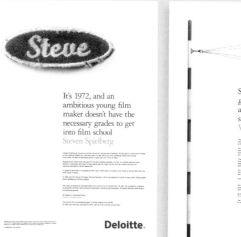

It's 1972, and an
ambitious young film
maker doesn't have the
necessary grades to get
into film school
Steven Spielberg

Deloitte.

Sometimes the non-
glamorous lab work is
absolutely crucial to the
success of a project
Wilbur Wright

Deloitte.

I was never one to obsess
about the past. Too much
to do in the future!
Sir Edmund Hillary

Deloitte.

Every time you follow the
lines on a metro map, you
have electrical engineering
to thank
Harry Beck

Deloitte.

We must become the
change we want to see
Mahatma Gandhi

Deloitte.

If you have zest and
enthusiasm you attract
zest and enthusiasm. Life
does give back in kind
Norman Vincent Peale

Deloitte.

I am a great
believer in luck,
and I find the
harder I work
the more I have
of it
Thomas Jefferson

Deloitte.

Rise above
A better view of
where to
compete

Deloitte.

Powers of
attraction
Identify, engage
and retain the
best people

Deloitte.

See the
opportunities
Play with
foresight

Deloitte.

Loud and proud
Deloitte-branded interior posters are not
throw-away items; they are invaluable
engagement tools, carefully designed to
communicate key messages.

One day,
one client
**Let's go out
for lunch**

Deloitte.

One day,
one client
**Take them out
for lunch**

Deloitte.

**A trash can...
Can say a lot
about your life**

Deloitte.

**Do you lock
your car door in
the morning?**
Then why don't
you lock your
computer?

Deloitte.

"I'm out of the office for
medical reasons. I will be
back in two weeks. Please
address me as Katryn
instead of Paul."
**Need inspiration for your
out of office reply?**

Deloitte.

**Contributing
to our clients'
success**
A different
perspective

Deloitte.

Don't let the
clock limit your
training
**Online Deloitte
training**

Deloitte.

Imagine the statue of
David without
Michelangelo
**The greatest ideas need
brilliant people**

Deloitte.

Imagine
Mona Lisa without
Leonardo da Vinci
**The greatest ideas need
brilliant people**

Deloitte.

Banana2000
Is that seriously
your password?

Deloitte.

Do you think
government is
boring?
**The Government
Get-2-Gether**

Deloitte.

Having visions is not the
same as having a vision
**Ours is to be the standard
of excellence**

Deloitte.

Good and badminton
The London office of the Deloitte UK member firm used conventional sports objects in unconventional ways, building them into their design motif to highlight their sponsorship of the Olympics in a bold, provocative fashion.

Events and exhibitions

Ornamental or organic? If the brand is more than logo, color, and type, then a corporate event or exhibition should be more than that as well. Instead of papering walls with the conventional and expected visual markers, envelop your audience in a truly—and deeply— branded experience.

Events and exhibitions are ideal occasions to promote B2B brands. They are a rare fusion of the organization's tangible and intangible assets, and they bring its professionals into direct contact with the audience. Whether via corporate roundtable, seminar series, analyst forum, or recruitment fair, there is an opportunity to make a strong impression on both conscious and subconscious levels.

The key to success? Brand immersion. This shouldn't be confused with brand submersion—audiences drowning in a sea of logos and trifold brochures. Brand immersion means engaging audiences in a rich, well-defined experience relevant to both the brand and the individual. The biggest failing of those attempting to create an effective event experience? A short-sighted, surface-level definition of *event*.

From the first mention of the gathering (e.g., e-mailed save-the-date, social-media notice, hard-copy invitation) to the last (e.g., thank-you e-mail, gift of appreciation, follow-up survey), the audience should be transported. The theme must be interesting, relevant, and communicated distinctly and consistently.

We like to create an impact on our audience through our events, key touchpoints within the total brand experience. We do this by ensuring a seamless Distinctly Deloitte experience, enabled by innovation and leadership.

MARC DE MAEYER
Marketing Director
Deloitte Belgium

Because Deloitte is a service brand, every opportunity to make it tangible is maximized. Events and exhibitions are important opportunities for converting the idea of the brand to real, distinctive, and memorable experiences. When Deloitte brand managers—all the people of Deloitte member firms—interact with clients, recruits, analysts, and other stakeholders, they are accomplishing something far greater than what might be achieved through a brochure or website. Therefore, events are never treated as afterthoughts; they are always given the same extensive resources, careful planning, and detailed execution as any brand-building moment.

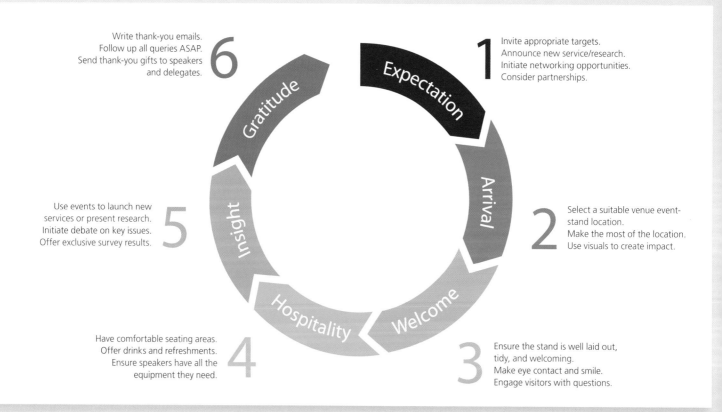

6 Write thank-you emails. Follow up all queries ASAP. Send thank-you gifts to speakers and delegates.

Gratitude

1 Expectation — Invite appropriate targets. Announce new service/research. Initiate networking opportunities. Consider partnerships.

5 Use events to launch new services or present research. Initiate debate on key issues. Offer exclusive survey results.

Insight

Arrival

2 Select a suitable venue event-stand location. Make the most of the location. Use visuals to create impact.

4 Have comfortable seating areas. Offer drinks and refreshments. Ensure speakers have all the equipment they need.

Hospitality

Welcome

3 Ensure the stand is well laid out, tidy, and welcoming. Make eye contact and smile. Engage visitors with questions.

In the event of an event
A six-step guide for an optimally branded experience.

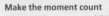

Make the moment count
Whatever the event or exhibition, Deloitte member firms strive to create memorable experiences and use the available time and budget to ensure that audiences are impressed.

Merchandise

If you're planning for a logo on a mouse pad, mug, or pen, you're about to waste a tremendous opportunity. Branded merchandise and promotional items beyond the ordinary have become strategic assets for the B2B marketer, helping savvy organizations make a statement—and a memory.

Merchandise allows an organization to connect at an emotional level not often attainable with traditional marketing and communication material. Branded items are portable and lasting brand impressions. Unlike pieces of marketing collateral that are quickly discarded or added to an ever-growing stack of paper in a bottom drawer, a smartly conceived and designed piece of merchandise can literally have an extended shelf life. Whether used as part of a direct mail campaign, an accompaniment to a high-profile announcement, or at a recruiting fair, merchandise can reinforce visual identity and distinguish a company from its competition.

Merchandise buying tips for "u"

- **Understandable:** There is an obvious reason why this item is coming from this organization.

- **Utility:** It has some degree of functionality and can somehow help the audience.

- **Unique:** It is unlike anything else the audience have seen or possess.

- **Unexpected:** It is not the conventional convention-type item.

- **Ultimate:** If it is like other items, it is best of breed.

- **Us:** It speaks not just to audience, but to their relationship with the brand.

What constitutes "smart" merchandise?

- **Appropriateness:** Is it suitable to the context and the recipient?

- **Style:** Is it of a high enough quality to be associated with the brand?

- **Authenticity:** Is it a realistic extension of the organization?

- **Design:** Can a logo or other brand identifier(s) be applied to the merchandise or its packaging?

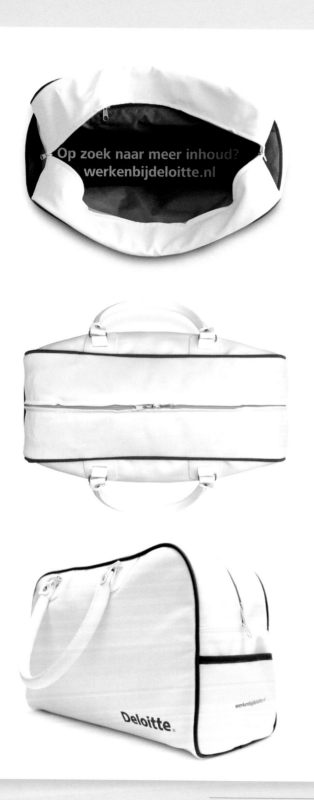

Many Deloitte member firms have corporate merchandise stores, with an assortment of branded items categorized by form, function, and cost. The majority of these employ the three elements in the B2B brand toolbox: logo, color, and typography. The omnipresent Deloitte logo can only appear against a white, blue, black, wood, or metallic item. Governing the application of these guidelines to merchandise is the principle of "focus," which informs design. This yields branded items that are understated and classic.

There are three types of Deloitte gifts:

- A **give-away** offered on event days as a token of appreciation. These useful, everyday items or foods are sometimes coupled with clever messaging or a distinctive design.

- A **branded gift** tailored to either specific events or individuals; bespoke messaging is standard.

- A **nonbranded gift** or premium item that has strong associations with a manufacturer's brand (e.g., a Hermès scarf). As it would be inappropriate to apply the Deloitte logo directly to this type of gift, it is packaged in a Deloitte-branded gift box or bag instead.

Gifts, give-aways, wearables—all are excellent means of conveying the Deloitte brand in a personal and memorable way. They should be treated as any other high-impact brand application.

JOSE MARIA ESTEBANEZ
Brand manager
Deloitte Spain

Logo on the go
Branded gifts provide an organization's people, clients, and recruits with a tangible "thank-you" while also portably promoting for a brand.

Green Dot Campaign style
Though not the norm, the number of Deloitte-branded wares produced without the Deloitte logo has increased. This rise reflects widespread recognition of the brand and a belief that, in some cases, the best way to stand out is to stand down. The most visible example of this "unbranded branding" is a T-shirt that features the graphics found in Deloitte's Green Dot Campaign ads.

No matter how strong the system, its effectiveness is ultimately determined by the active management of a centralized team, in concert with a globally shared desire to foster the brand.

Defending it

Brand asset management

It takes several months to create a multifaceted system of brand elements and applications, but it requires years of strategic implementation and activation to achieve market penetration and recognition. The management of all brand assets is no less important than the assets themselves.

A comprehensive and clear asset management strategy can ensure their proper use by internal professionals and authorized external parties alike. It can also mitigate improper use by those who neither speak nor act on behalf of the organization.

The most common and most effective mechanism for housing, organizing, and safeguarding this intellectual property is a centralized brand-content repository. Though the scale can vary, the minimum requirements for such a hub include a listing of all core elements, general guidelines for their application, and a download section. A centrally managed database can also facilitate periodic audits of the brand assets and changes to the system.

One site for one brand
Brand Space is the online asset management system for the Deloitte master brand. Employees as well as authorized vendors and agencies visit the database approximately 40,000 times per month.

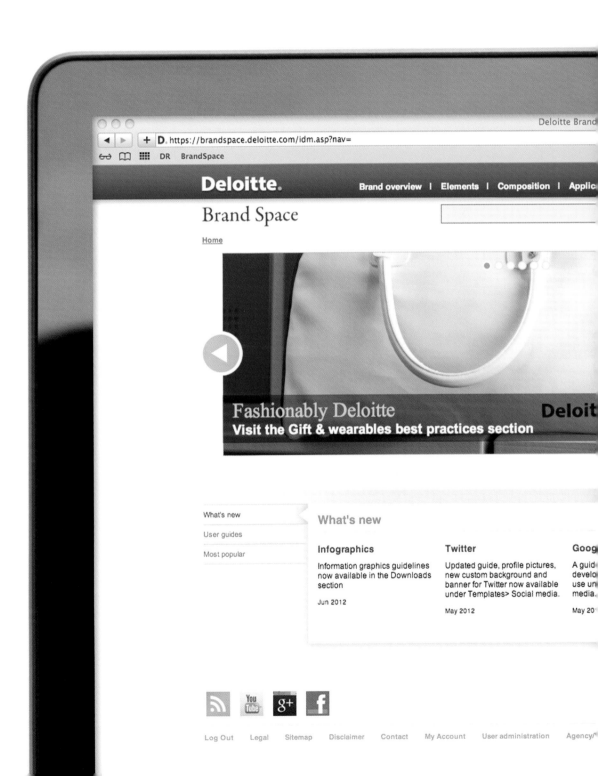

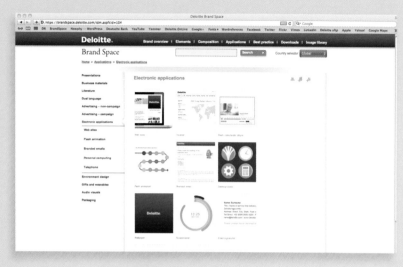

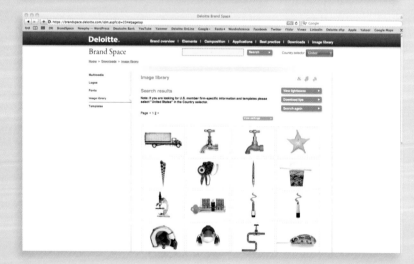

Upping the brand with downloads
Brand Space houses a comprehensive library of downloadable assets ranging from logos to templates to an image bank of more than 1,500 royalty-free photos.

The epicenter of Deloitte's global brand asset management effort is Brand Space, an online repository of content that is accessible by all Deloitte member firm professionals, as well as approved vendors and agencies. Hundreds of pages of guidelines for the application of core elements are supplemented by a best-practices gallery, rights-cleared stock photography, and a comprehensive template library. Additionally, there is extensive language detailing the bones of the brand—its strategic framework and how it connects to business objectives.

Managing brand assets is not the responsibility of a handful of brand champions, but of the entire organization, from practice professionals to marketing personnel to executive assistants.

MICHAEL GRABISH
Design Director, Brand, Communications & Community
Deloitte United States

About our brand

Brand attributes

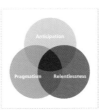

Always One Step Ahead.

Brand positioning

Deloitte.

Primary logo

The brand four pillars

Play.

Market messages

Brand architecture

Color palette

Global endorsement

Industries

Consumer Business
Energy and Resources
Life Sciences and Healthcare
Manufacturing
Public Sector
Real Estate
Technology and Media

Industry programs

Functions

Audit
Consulting
Financial Advisory
Tax

Functions

Headlines
Garamond
3 LT std

Frutiger Next Pro
Bold headlines

**Frutiger Next Pro
Light bodycopy**

Typography

Brand vs. legal name

*i*Zone
*i*Café
*i*Know

Brand building initiatives

DeepDive™
The ultimate
collaboration tool

Proprietary products

Imagery

Xtend **Deloitte.**

Xtend®
by **Deloitte.**

Branded acquisitions

SUPPORTED BY

Deloi

Sponsorships

The chemistry
of talent
New ways to think
about people and
work

Tone of voice

Music

Paréntesis

Printed applications

Electronic applications

1

Advertising

Environments

Setting a new standard
Deloitte standards for brand identity,
design, and messaging are extensively
described on "Brand Space," with all
guidelines categorized by element or
application.

Brand compliance

Enforcing compliance is essential for ensuring brand consistency, quality, and security. Those who lead this area—the "brand cops"—are often seen as obstructionist, and suffer, ironically, from a bad "brand." Fortunately, this perception can be altered, but doing so requires promoting a deeper understanding of branding, business, and most importantly, behaviors.

Brand compliance should be viewed as the end, not the means. Focusing first on building an alliance will make it easier to achieve compliance. There will assuredly be instances when a heavier hand will be needed to ensure effective brand adoption—especially during identity-system launches and refreshes. But a light touch usually leads to the best results. Remember, many internal clients simply don't have the understanding of branding that the specialists possess. The ability to articulate the brand strategy simply, through a lens relevant to the business, can get all players on the same page.

For the launch of Deloitte's master brand strategy in 2003, a small, dedicated group oversaw the design, rollout, and implementation of the architecture and identity. Two brand managers from the global office of Deloitte Touche Tohmatsu Limited, supported primarily by select local-office marketing and communications professionals, focused on visual identity and a very literal, relatively strict interpretation of the newly created standards.

Over the years, the Global Brand team has increased in size and scope, as has its champion network; highly specialized brand leaders are now in place at most member firms, and the original one-way, operational approach has given way to one distinguished by collaboration and consultation.

Auditing the auditors
In 2007, the Global Brand team of Deloitte Touche Tohmatsu Limited conducted an internal brand audit of a wide range of material from member firms from over 100 countries.

Ten laws for the brand cop

1. **Be nice.** People expect compliance professionals to be hard-edged, and unanticipated kindness and empathy can disarm your audience.

2. **Be human.** Cold, black-and-white communications from faceless, nameless e-mail accounts neither engender trust nor compel people to change their ways.

3. **Build relationships.** Once you have established contact, stay connected; people are less likely to go off-brand if they feel their actions not only have implications for the business, but are appreciated by individuals.

4. **Educate.** Use every interaction as a teaching opportunity, illustrating not just the right way, but how and why it is correct.

5. **Consultation over compliance.** Position yourself as expert adviser rather than enforcer; be positive and constructive, working toward mutually satisfactory outcomes.

6. **Flexibility is critical.** Brand guidelines are usually just that: guidelines, not black-and-white rules; find ways to accommodate audience needs through astute interpretations of the standards.

7. **Present options.** Work with people to unearth the core idea they are trying to express, and use your own resources to better align it with the brand.

8. **Opt to present.** Rather than sending simple e-mails in response to higher-profile queries and requests, create presentations that vividly illustrate the solution; this can lead to increasing the audience's understanding.

9. **ABC:** Always Be Closing. Every communication should focus on achieving your end goal, and the audience should feel good about, or at least comfortable with, that result.

10. **Escalate.** The "nuclear option" is an elevation of the issue to leadership; as the brand strategy is tied to the business and likely endorsed by the C-suite, turning to executives for support (or simply expressing a willingness to do so) can be a persuasive incentive.

Brand compliance is more effective when our professionals understand why elements are in place and why it is to their advantage to use them appropriately. Simply memorizing guidelines, while it may lead to strict consistency, may not provide the leeway to develop effective communications.

JOHN KELLER
Brand, Communications & Corporate Citizenship
Deloitte United States

Brand champions

Every employee, whether they know it or not, is responsible for shaping their B2B company's brand. But only a fraction are true brand champions. The difference is one that does not appear in most job descriptions or on most resumes: passion.

Titles such as *brand manager* and *visual identity director* usually describe full-time, clearly defined, exclusively focused roles. The more nebulous *brand champion* should not, however, be mistaken as the title of someone lacking import or influence. Just the opposite. That an organization's brand champions are off the payroll (that is, as regards this function) and agenda-free imbues their efforts with increased authenticity and power.

B2Cs are heavily reliant upon brand ambassadors and other third-party sponsors compensated specifically for communicating and demonstrating the brand's value. B2B brand champions literally live the brand. They serve as stewards and evangelists. And while they often preach, it is usually their actions, and not their words, that inspire allegiance. Their very actions should define the brand values and lead to an increase in enthusiasm among their peers.

Deloitte's brand champion network is comprised of hundreds of professionals who lead by example; they include not just Deloitte member firm professionals but also vendors and even clients who bring the brand attributes to life every day. Though no formal certification program exists, this group is recognized by the central Brand and Communications group and treated as extended members of the team. While they assist with certain local compliance activities, they are counted on more for inspiring brand-aligned action.

The driving force behind any successful brand story is always people. A powerful strategy and effective tools can only do so much. In the end, it's your people who embody your brand's credentials.

CATHY BENKO
Vice Chairman and Managing Principal
Brand, Communications and Corporate Citizenship
Deloitte United States

Tips for cultivating brand champions among employees

- Conduct an immersive brand training that exposes them to brand positioning and attributes.
- Promote an inclusive environment in which they can contribute to shaping and evolving the brand.
- Communicate the need for brand alignment through goals and performance.
- Empower them with a supplemental title and the responsibility to enforce brand consistency.
- Equip them with branded items and merchandise that enables them to literally carry the brand.

Tips for cultivating brand champions among executive management

- Reinforce the need for consistency in messaging and behavior.
- Lead by example, as their decisions have a direct impact on brand legacy and will ripple throughout the organization.
- Provide cheat sheets for brand messaging and positioning for all communications.
- Ensure information flows downward to employees smoothly and frequently: every decision impacts the brand.
- Audit the brand periodically to identify strengths and inconsistencies.

Brand Champions

Though Brand Space automates brand management, providing the requisite tools to those responsible for shaping the Deloitte brand, small teams of brand-focused professionals at the global and local levels provide additional guidance and aid in resolving any conflicts.

Tips for cultivating brand champions among clients

- Make interaction as personal and authentic as possible.
- Encourage them to tell your story in their own words, from their own experiences.
- Communicate brand enhancements and amendments clearly and frequently.
- Employ surveys, polls, and testimonials to capture client insights related to brand perceptions.
- Address any problems clients have quickly, transparently, and with integrity.
- Provide branded merchandise and apparel.
- Develop reward and recognition programs.

Tips for cultivating brand champions among agencies, vendors, and suppliers

- Provide access to your brand asset management system and/or related foundational material.
- Explain their responsibilities as key shapers and influencers of the brand.
- Ensure their understanding of organizational culture and its intangible properties.
- Furnish them with a brand and identity checklist or other tools to ensure they are aligned with the brand and understand its optimal expression.
- Be certain they are versed in corporate policies around business ethics, as they serve as extensions of the organization.

Designers and networks

Though rarely credited as top-line B2B brand-builders, designers are among the most influential shapers of perceptions and behaviors. They are able to translate complex words into compelling ideas, bridging the gap between an organization and its audiences in vibrant, meaningful, and differentiated ways.

B2B brands are messaged via an array of marketing and communications vehicles. A common denominator: they all must be designed. The organization's graphic design professionals must therefore understand the content, the feedback of internal clients, and how to articulate that information within the identity system. Designers are responsible for turning the factual into the conceptual, balancing imagination with a keen understanding of how to best express the brand promise. Their importance requires a company to develop a design force that is technically skilled, creative, and well versed in the brand.

Among the first to learn and experiment with new techniques, technologies, and channels of communication, designers are on the front lines of innovation. Their experience and perspectives make them an invaluable internal focus group and test panel with the ability to influence the direction of the corporate brand.

Harnessing this intelligence will not only promote the brand's identifications with forward-thinking generally; it will also greatly aid talent retention: more than most employees, designers strive to be part of a progressive and stimulating environment.

Deloitte's official designer network is comprised of approximately 500 professionals. They are not communicated to; they are communicated with. Through dialoguing channels like Yammer, as well as monthly conference calls, they exchange ideas and share best practices. Such interaction is key to elevating the brand identity organically. Designers are also encouraged to "borrow with pride," and so apply to their local markets what has proven effective in others.

Our cross-regional brand consistency can be attributed to a shared culture, and that includes a shared culture of creativity. Our designers are constantly leading by example and pushing Deloitte to new levels.

ANDRES ESPINOSA
Director, Brand and Marketing (LATCO)
Deloitte Colombia

Design thinking
Visual aids help to bring the Deloitte brand to life—and not just in brochures and presentations. Design is used to add personality to the brand, enriching the brand experience of all who interact with it.

Creative Studio, London
Specially equipped spaces such
as these turn Deloitte offices
into agency-like environments
with a focus on collaborative and
creative thinking.

Rollout strategies

The most effective B2B brand *rollout* strategies have clear *role in* strategies—with everyone in the organization understanding their essential role in the launch and active management of the brand. Regardless of the scope of the brand work, or the scale of the organization, synchronicity and stewardship are always imperative.

Before a rollout strategy can be created, it must be abundantly clear what, exactly, it is in support of. This question raises others: Is this the launch of a new positioning platform? A comprehensive campaign to reflect a defined purpose? A completely refreshed visual identity system? Or a combination of these? The answer must be viewed through the lens of the brand architecture and organizational construct: the look and feel of a master-brand rollout will be quite different from that of a family of endorsed businesses.

Once the nature of the launch is understood and its budget has been determined, the strategy and corresponding tactics should begin to take form. Interestingly, the focal points for internal and external brand rollouts will likely be very similar. Articulating brand differentiation, benefits, and value, and doing it all in an engaging, personalized manner, transcends the client-employee divide. Audiences—including even a company's own people—will be asking, "What's in it for me?" and responses need to be strong, succinct, and supportable.

A challenging rollout

To support the launch of the Green Dot Campaign—the biggest international external communications effort in the history of the Deloitte brand—the Green Dot Challenge was devised. The engagement initiative invited internal and external audiences to come up with their own advertisements using a custom online tool.

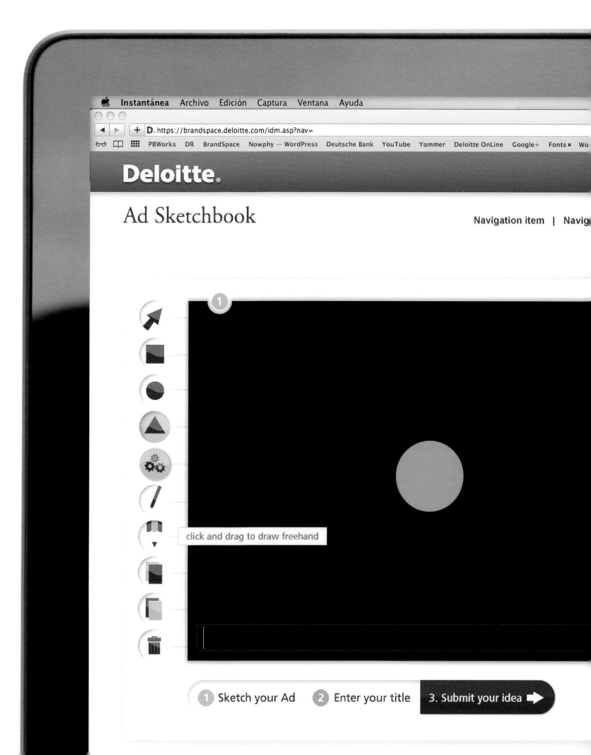

Why take risks?

Deloitte.

Be the start of the crescendo

Deloitte.

And the winner is...
The contest received thousands of submissions. The entries displayed a wonderful mix of creativity, insight, and understanding of the Deloitte brand. Three winners were selected, representing the Americas, Asia-Pacific, and Europe-Middle East-Africa regions.

Re-design your business for the future

Deloitte.

It may take many months for this question to be answered fully. So even if you opt for a big-bang launch rather than an incremental, phased rollout, the messaging must remain before the audience. Respect the fine line between embedding and oversaturating, and make certain that every communication is relevant.

It's always tempting to focus on the campaigns or the products when you roll out a brand strategy, but the people in your own organization are your best asset. Bring them along first, and everything else will fall in place.

SUZANNE GYLFE
Director, Marketing & Brand
Deloitte United States

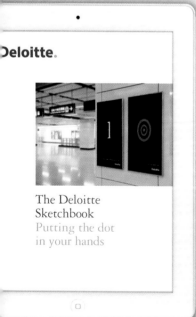

The Deloitte
Sketchbook
Putting the dot
in your hands

How high are your aims?

Deloitte.

Kits are serious business

Whether launching a B2B brand, repositioning it, or reshaping its identity, a rollout kit can greatly enhance internal stakeholder engagement, understanding, and stewardship. In addition to hard-copy or electronic distribution, consider including the following:

- **(Hi)story of the brand.** Illustrate the brand journey and the people behind it.

- **Brand one-pager.** Draw up a summary sheet featuring brand architecture, positioning, attributes, and personality.

- **Memory cards.** Feature all core brand components as part of an integrated set.

- **Links.** Include all relevant URLs and QR codes

- **Core templates.** Include the most common applications, and embed visual identity assets.

- **Video.** Add personality, emotion, and sensory elements to the brand.

- **Merchandise.** Ensure it is fun, or functional—or both—and unmistakably branded.

- **Contest/incentivized activity.** Develop an engagement exercise to build community and raise spirits.

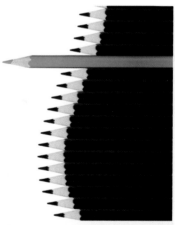

Promo it with the promo kit

To help Deloitte member firms activate the program locally, a promotional kit was developed centrally and distributed to each country's brand champions. It included posters, magazine ads, online banners, e-communication templates, and even placemats.

Workshops and education

External permeation begins with internal education. From executive-level training on messaging to designer-specific immersion in the visual identity, a well-executed brand education program can significantly increase the network of brand champions and boost the understanding and enthusiasm of all employees.

Thinking about brand education means thinking about brand experience. Many of the lessons in enhancing the brand experience—making it memorable, making it actionable, making it easy to relate to—are equally applicable to the enhancement of brand skills and awareness. And as with shaping the brand experience, there is no replacement for face-to-face interaction. The personal touch not only fosters personal and emotional connections; it begins to establish a genuine relationship between the brand executive and the brand executers. The bond formed is invaluable and results in an extended team for which brand compliance is not an obligation or headache, but a responsibility and point of pride.

Workshop modeling is a crucial part of the educational process. Begin by focusing content and approach to the audience. There is power in both cross-functional workshops, in which employees can see how their assorted specializations can come together for a holistic brand experience, as well as in more role-specific sessions. If possible, develop a theme beyond the brand itself—an engaging, "gettable" idea that will become a common thread for the entire presentation. It can even be extended beyond the workshop to follow-up communications and actions. Finally, and most critically, at every training, be sure to convey not just the what, where, when, and how of the brand, but also the why of the brand—its essence and the reasons an organization and its people should care.

Deloitte.

Why are brands important?

Now imagine that there were several alternative providers of these products and services, some similarly priced, others differently priced, but you were unable to tell which goods came from which source. How would you decide which to choose?

49   50   99

MacBook Pro

The Global Brand team of Deloitte Touche Tohmatsu Limited regularly leads in-person workshops for member firms in priority markets. These sessions, which range from broad brand inductions to more specific discussions around positioning, engagement, and visual identity, sometimes serve as "train the trainer" sessions. They equip member-firm brand, marketing, and communications professionals to facilitate similar workshops on a local level. To ensure the widest reach—both in geography and subject matter—monthly conference calls feature comprehensive brand updates. Finally, an online training module is accessible by all 195,000 professionals, providing a high-level overview of the Deloitte brand and how it can be brought to life.

B2B branding, P2P training
Face-to-face or "person-to-person" training sessions are commonplace at the Deloitte member firms, where they are facilitated by professionals from the Global Brand team and country brand champions.

Most of our leaders didn't really get the concept of "brand" until the workshops. These sessions became the tipping point, where the "aha" moments happened and the passion for our brand was ignited.

KENT KIRCH
Global Director of Talent Acquisition & Mobility
Deloitte Touche Tohmatsu Limited

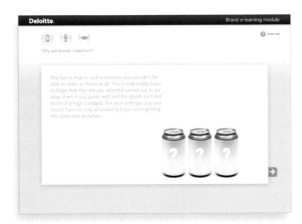

Align, online
A custom online training module is used for the brand orientation of Deloitte member firm professionals. Easily accessible and easily consumable, it enables all employees to acquire a basic comprehension of branding, what it means at Deloitte, and what it means for them.

Learning to lead
Deloitte University, a cutting-edge facility in Texas, is a learning environment that allows the people of the Deloitte U.S. member firm to inspire one another and spark insightful thinking—to "lead from the front."

Evolving the system

Emerging technologies, vacillating audience behavior, and shifting business strategies all represent significant challenges—and opportunities—for B2B brand managers. To prepare for the inevitable, formulate an identity system flexible enough to shape both the leading brand of today and the leading-edge brand of tomorrow.

Static brands quickly become stale. For dynamic brands, some of their maturation will be organic, as the actions of stakeholders both inside and outside the organization naturally influence direction and perceptions. But a more calculated approach to brand evolution is required, and should be considered during the earliest stages of identity development.

As we have grown, so has the size, depth, and flexibility of Deloitte's identity system. This has allowed us to realize our potential and connect with our clients.

SACHIYO KIKUCHI
Senior Manager, Clients and Industries
Deloitte Japan

Since the formal refresh and relaunch of its identity system in 2008, the Deloitte brand has continued to grow. New service lines and offices have emerged to meet member firms' needs, and new manifestations of the core design elements have resulted in a host of fresh applications to better connect with the audience. Not surprisingly, many of these fall within the digital arena, where rapidly emerging technologies are driving brand consumption; these include tools, templates, and guidance for audiovisual treatments, infographics, and social-media presence.

Another key enhancement to the Deloitte brand system was the "custom identity build," which enables signature groups, programs, and initiatives to develop mini-brands. Notable for their tailored verbal and visual expressions, these identities allow areas of strategic priority to communicate with particular markets clearly and consistently without undermining the master brand. They support the broader system while also differentiating themselves from other parts of the organization.

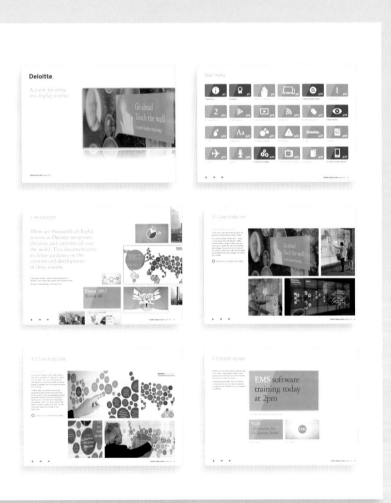

Mind the gap
Make sure your B2B brand includes guidance around the following:

- Communicating through, and designing for, social-media channels
- Apps
- Motion graphics in video
- Infographics
- Mobile-friendly templates
- Digital publishing
- Interactive devices, such a iPhones and touch-screen walls
- QR and Snap codes
- Alternative presentation formats such as Keynote and Prezl

Staying in touch
New guidance on how to optimize interactive touch screens and signage is keeping the brand fresh and audiences engaged.

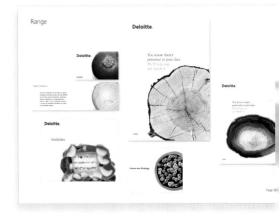

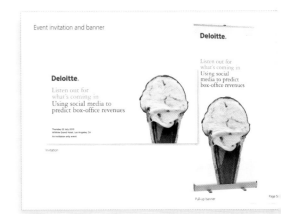

Looking into change
Bespoke identities for service offerings such as Deloitte Analytics are enabling the member firms to connect with clients in deeper, more memorable ways.

Image credits

Page IV, [Cars]: © Deloitte Belgium
Page V, [Cars]: © Deloitte Belgium
Page VI, [Deloitte group]: © Deloitte Global Services Limited
Page IX, [Heather Hancock]: © Deloitte United Kingdom
Page 3, [Laboratory]: © Stephen Smith / Photodisc / Getty Images
Page 4, [Boy holding a poster]: © Deloitte Australia
Page 7, [Test tubes]: © Horiyan / Shutterstock.com
Page 8, [Books]: © Lauren Nicole / Photographer's Choice RF / Getty Images
Page 8, [Name Tag]: © C Squared Studios / Photodisc / Getty Images
Page 9, [Trunk]: © Deloitte Global Services Limited (Deloitte Analytics)
Page 9, [Truckload]: © Deloitte Global Services Limited (Deloitte Analytics)
Page 9, [Watering can]: © Deloitte Global Services Limited (Deloitte Analytics)
Page 11, [Metal hook]: © Volodymyr Krasyuk / Shutterstock.com
Page 12, [Shoes and socks]: © Deloitte Australia
Page 14, [Green grass]: © Nopporn0510 / Shutterstock.com
Page 15, [Green grass]: © Nopporn0510 / Shutterstock.com
Page 15, [Hot air balloon]: © Vividz Foto / Shutterstock.com
Page 17, [Table and armchairs in modern office]: © Serp / Shutterstock.com
Page 19, [Boy with a cup]: © Deloitte Australia
Page 21, [Brand arquitecture]: © Deloitte Global Services Limited
Page 25, [Torn paper with hole]: © iStockphoto.com / AntiMartina
Page 27, [Corridor]: © Deloitte Global Services Limited. Photography by Thomas Oswald
Page 27, [Corridor]: © Deloitte Global Services Limited. Photography by Thomas Oswald
Page 28, [Always One Step Ahead iPad app]: © Photography by Andy Mac
Page 29, [Always One Step Ahead book]: © Photography by Andy Mac
Page 31, [Brand experience screenshot]: © Deloitte Global Services Limited
Page 31, [Ad in subway]: © TungCheung / Shutterstock.com
Page 31, [Deloitte car]: © Deloitte Belgium
Page 31, [Barry Salzberg, Office screen]: © Deloitte Global Services Limited
Page 32, [Touchpoints]: © Deloitte Global Services Limited
Page 32, [Stakeholders wheel]: © Deloitte Global Services Limited
Page 33, [Keys of a calculator disarmed]: © Rafael Angel Garcia Dobarganes / Shutterstock.com
Page 33, [MacBook Pro]: © RTimages / Alamy
Page 33, [Apple iPhone 4s]: © Oleksiy Maksymenko / Alamy
Page 33, [Brand experience screenshots]: © Deloitte Global Services Limited
Page 35, [Ride Across Britain images]: © Threshold Sports
Page 36, [Ride Across Britain images]: © Threshold Sports
Page 37, [Ride Across Britain images]: © Threshold Sports
Page 39, [Chilli]: © Kuznetsov Alexey / Shutterstock.com
Page 40, [Stethoscope]: © Lusoimages - Health / Alamy
Page 40, [Powerpoint Slides]: © Millward Brown data, 2011
Page 41, [Protractor]: © Datacraft Co Ltd / Getty Images
Page 45, [Name tag]: © C Squared Studios / Photodisc / Getty Images
Page 46, [Deloitte logos]: © Deloitte Global Services Limited
Page 47, [Name tag]: © iStockphoto.com / Devonyu
Page 50, [Global Business Tax Services]: © Photography by David Arky
Page 50, [Middle Market]: © Jag_cz / Shutterstock.com
Page 50, [Deloitte Analytics]: © Deloitte Global Services Limited (Deloitte Analytics)
Page 50, [Knowledge Management]: © Photography by David Arky
Page 50, [Alumni Network]: © Photography by David Arky
Page 50, [Pens]: © Stockbyte / Getty Images
Page 53, [Corridor]: © Deloitte Global Services Limited. Photography by Thomas Oswald
Page 57, [Deloitte logo]: © Deloitte Global Services Limited
Page 59, [Deloitte signage Melbourne]: © Deloitte Australia
Page 61, [Paintbrush]: © The Partners
Page 63, [Artichoke]: © Deloitte Global Services Limited (Deloitte Analytics)
Page 63, [Ludo DeKeulenaer]: © Deloitte Global Services Limited
Page 65, [Brochure]: © Deloitte Global Services Limited
Page 68, [Wires]: © Photography by Andy Mac
Page 69, [Wind measurement tool]: © Photography by Andy Mac
Page 70, [Colorful powder]: © thefinalmiracle / Shutterstock.com
Page 70, [Green sphere]: © valdis torms / Shutterstock.com
Page 71, [Sofa]: © Deloitte United Kingdom
Page 71, [Rear View Mirror]: © Ryan McVay / Photodisc / Getty Images
Page 71, [Buttons Link magazine]: © Deloitte Global Services Limited
Page 71, [Life magazine]: © Deloitte Touche Tohmatsu Limited
Page 71, [Snow texture with foot prints]: © Dudarev Mikhail / Shutterstock.com
Page 71, [Deloitte executives]: © Deloitte United Kingdom
Page 73, [Monkey wrench]: © The Partners
Page 75, [Water splash]: © Phant / Shutterstock.com
Page 75, [Measuring device]: © The Partners
Page 75, [Tree]: ukmooney / Shutterstock.com
Page 77, [Icons]: © The Partners
Page 78, [Federal budget icons]: © Deloitte Australia
Page 79, [Icons]: © Deloitte Global Services Limited
Page 79, [White iPad]: © Oleksiy Maksymenko Photography / Alamy
Page 81, [Twitter infographic]: © Deloitte United States
Page 82, [Infographics]: © Deloitte Global Services Limited
Page 83, [Football Money League Infographic]: © Deloitte United Kingdom

Page 83, [Annual Review Football Finance Infographic]: © Deloitte United Kingdom
Page 85, [Sound waveform]: © swillklitch / Shutterstock.com
Page 86, [Deloitte logo animation]: © Motion504
Page 87, [Audio logo notes]: © Deloitte Global Services Limited
Page 87, [deFilharmonie logo]: © deFilharmonie
Page 87, [Musicians]: © deFilharmonie / Photography by Bert Hulselmans
Page 91, [Blank white paper]: © Picsfive / Shutterstock.com
Page 92, [Stationery]: © Deloitte Global Services Limited
Page 93, [Stationery]: © Deloitte Global Services Limited
Page 95, [MacBook Pro]: © S K D / Alamy
Page 96, [Prezi - Magnifying glass]: © Vitaly Korovin / Shutterstock.com
Page 96, [Keynote - iPad]: © Anatolii Babii / Alamy
Page 96, [Report screenshots]: © Deloitte Global Services Limited
Page 97, [MacBook Pro]: © RTimages / Alamy
Page 97, [Digital Tablet PC]: © ArtBabii / Alamy
Page 97, [Prezi screenshot]: © Prezi Inc.
Page 99, [Selection of brochures]: © Art Directors & TRIP / Alamy
Page 99, [Ceiling fan]: © Deloitte United Kingdom
Page 99, [Toothpaste tube]: © Deloitte Belgium
Page 99, [Suitcases]: © Deloitte Germany
Page 99, [Chocolate stain]: © Deloitte Belgium
Page 99, [Clocks on a basket]: © Deloitte Brazil
Page 99, [Slized apple]: © Deloitte Brazil
Page 99, [Wires]: © Deloitte Spain
Page 100, [Old shoe]: © Deloitte Germany
Page 100, [Key]: © Deloitte Germany
Page 100, [Pencil]: © Deloitte Germany
Page 100, [Rocket]: © Deloitte Germany
Page 100, [Deloitte Mini Cooper]: © Deloitte Belgium
Page 100, [Snowboarder]: © fotum / Shutterstock.com
Page 101, [A4 third brochures]: © Deloitte Middle East. Design by Communication Design s.a.l.
Page 101, [Transfer Pricing brochure]: © Deloitte Germany
Page 103, [The Pod magazine]: © Deloitte Singapore
Page 103, [Solventia magazine]: © Deloitte Spain
Page 103, [Deloitte Matters magazine]: © Deloitte Belgium
Page 103, [Link magazine]: © Deloitte Germany
Page 103, [Dialog magazine]: © Deloitte Germany
Page 103, [Up front magazine]: © Deloitte United Kingdom
Page 104, [Mundo Corporativo magazine]: © Deloitte Brazil
Page 104, [POV magazine]: © Deloitte Middle East. Design by Communication Design s.a.l.
Page 105, [Punto de vista newspaper]: © Deloitte Spain
Page 106, [Green Sphere]: © The Partners
Page 107, [Annual Review cover]: © The Partners
Page 108, [Leading the field Review]: © Deloitte United Kingdom
Page 108, [An open book Review]: © © Deloitte United Kingdom
Page 108, [Tablet PC and Mobile smartphone]: © ArtBabii / Alamy
Page 109, [Interior of Annual Review]: © Deloitte Global Services Limited
Page 111, [Proposal packaging]: © Deloitte Spain
Page 112, [The proposal kit]: © Deloitte Global Services Limited
Page 115, [Green bowl]: © iStockphoto.com / Narcisa
Page 116, [Shopping in style]: © iStockphoto.com / DOConnell
Page 116, [CD packaging - Athletes]: © William Perugini / Shutterstock.com
Page 117, [Woman brand new shoe]: © fiphoto / Shutterstock.com
Page 117, [Ladies high heeled shoes]: © Kitch Bain / Shutterstock.com
Page 117, [White shopping bag]: © Feng Yu / Alamy
Page 117, [Carton box post package]: © Dmitriy Sechin / Alamy
Page 117, [Paper white bags]: © Aleksandr Volkov / Alamy
Page 119, [White calendar]: © Feng Yu / Alamy
Page 120, [Plug]: © Jonathan Kitchen / Digital Vision / Getty Images
Page 120, [Wires]: © Photography by Andy Mac
Page 121, [Forks]: © The Partners
Page 121, [Toast]: © The Partners
Page 121, [Wine]: © The Partners
Page 121, [Open book]: © Serg64 / Shutterstock.com
Page 121, [Yellow safety helmet]: © Taurus / Shutterstock.com
Page 121, [Speaker]: © Deloitte United Kingdom
Page 123, [Ad in newspaper]: © Deloitte Australia
Page 124, [Ad in airport]: © Deloitte Belgium
Page 124, [Ad in building]: © Deloitte Belgium
Page 124, [Ad in subway]: © TungCheung / Shutterstock.com
Page 125, [YouTube channel]: © Google, Inc. Used with permission.
Page 125, [Billboard - Stairs]: © iStockphoto.com / Parema
Page 125, [Newspaper - Top]: © Deloitte Australia
Page 125, [Winning banner]: © Deloitte United Kingdom
Page 125, [Cyber security ad]: © Deloitte United Kingdom (Cyber Security)
Page 126, [Advertisement guidelines]: © Deloitte Global Services Limited
Page 127, [Ads]: © Deloitte Global Services Limited. Created by The Partners and MuirHoward
Page 129, [IFA event Argentina]: © Deloitte Argentina
Page 129, [IFA event - Girls]: © Deloitte Argentina

The authors

... have the privilege of being the two longest tenured members of the Global Brand team of Deloitte Touche Tohmatsu Limited. During this time, we have collaborated with one another and with global and local leadership to transform the Deloitte brand identity, as well as the manner in which it is managed. The job has exposed us to complex, engaging disciplines. (Yes, audit and tax can in fact be quite stimulating). The job has allowed us to work closely with some of the world's finest people, as intelligent as they are interesting. The job has genuinely become more than a job...as it should be, for any Brand Manager worth his or her salt. We understand the responsibility placed upon us, and do not take it lightly. And hope that by sharing our perspectives and passion, some of it may rub off on our readers and their own brands.

Brian Resnick

Associate Director, Global Brand
Deloitte Touche Tohmatsu Limited

Brian is responsible for leading the area of brand activation and expression, worldwide. This encompasses the most high-profile components of the Deloitte brand — specifically, the visual identity, brand assets, and the myriad guidelines, tools, and templates created to deliver them in a consistent and quality manner. He has been a member of the Global Brand team since 2006, and spent the three years prior with the Deloitte U.S. member firm, focused on marketing and communications. Previously, he spent time working at American International Group and two boutique recruitment advertising agencies. Brian has had feature articles published in *Brandweek* and online blogs, and leads brand identity workshops around the world.

bresnick@deloitte.com

To my girls, Heather and Laura, and to my parents, for all they've put into me and all their putting up with me.

For comments or inquiries about *Designing B2B Brands*:
GlobalDesigningB2bBrands@deloitte.com

Carlos Martínez Onaindía

Senior Manager, Global Brand
Deloitte Touche Tohmatsu Limited

Carlos leads the Global Brand Studio, with a focus on developing brand assets, tools, and applications for the areas of brand expression, brand activation, and brand engagement. He also frequently serves as executive creative consultant on global initiatives, providing art direction across mediums. In addition to his global role, where he provides guidance around brand compliance and creative execution to member firms covering over 140 countries, he also designs custom identity packages for assorted Industry and Service Line practices. Carlos first joined the Deloitte network as the leader of graphic design and creativity for the Spanish member firm. He later transitioned to DTTL, where he's been a member of the Global Brand team since 2008.

cmartinezonaindia@deloitte.es

To Marta, Andrea, and Alessandro, my life team, and to my parents for supporting me every single moment of my life.

Index

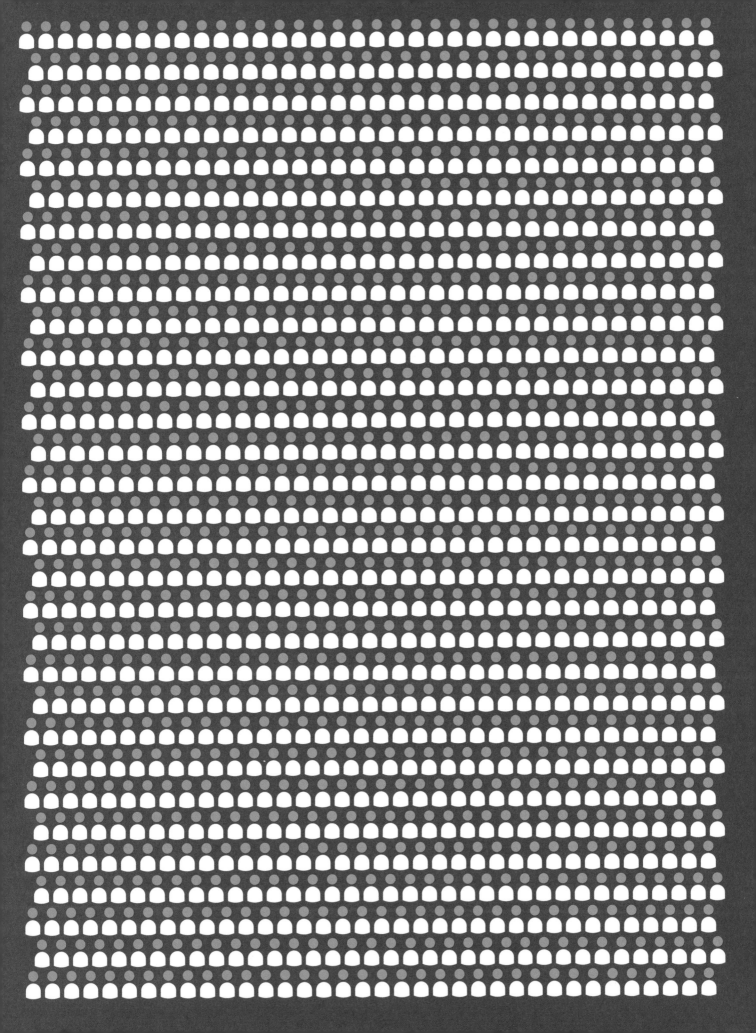

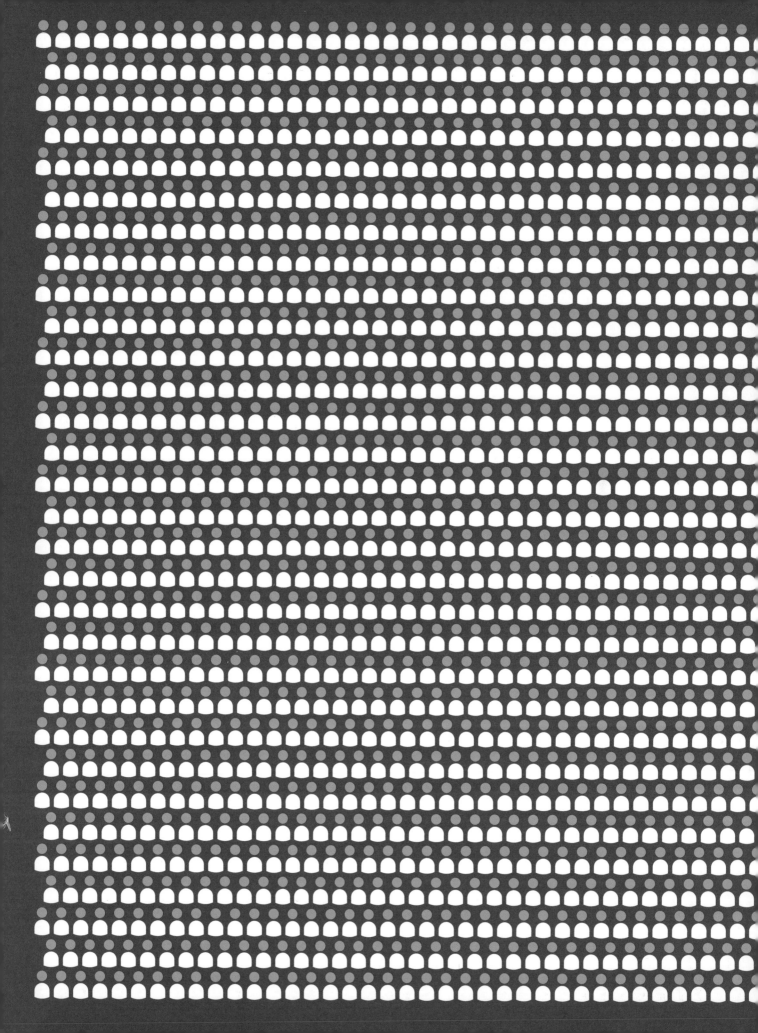